M000290024

A Year of
Angel
GUIDANCE

© Daniel_sahnn / Daniel Murillo-Vasquez

About the Author

Leeza Robertson has been seeking answers to her questions for as long as she can remember. She spent years developing her research skills in both her undergraduate and post graduate work at Melbourne University. Throughout her time in the academic stacks, she dreamed of one day having her works published. Now Leeza is the author of multiple publications on tarot and spiritual development, with books available in multiple languages across the globe. Visit her Patreon at: https://www.patreon.com/LeezaRobertson.

An INTRODUCTION to
TWELVE
NEW GUARDIANS

A Year of
Angel
GUIDANCE

LEEZA ROBERTSON

Author of *The Divine Practice of Angel Numbers*

Llewellyn Publications • Woodbury, Minnesota

LIBRARY OF
CONGRESS
SURPLUS
DUPLICATE

A Year of Angel Guidence: An Introduction to Twelve New Guardians © 2023 by Leeza Robertson. All rights reserved. No part of this book may be used or reproduced in any manner whatsoever, including internet usage, without written permission from Llewellyn Publications, except in the case of brief quotations embodied in critical articles and reviews.

FIRST EDITION
First Printing, 2023

Book design by Mandie Brasington
Cover design by Shannon McKuhen
Interior Illustrations by Llewellyn Art Department

Llewellyn Publications is a registered trademark of Llewellyn Worldwide Ltd.

Library of Congress Cataloging-in-Publication Data (Pending)
ISBN: 978-0-7387-7031-4

Llewellyn Worldwide Ltd. does not participate in, endorse, or have any authority or responsibility concerning private business transactions between our authors and the public.

All mail addressed to the author is forwarded but the publisher cannot, unless specifically instructed by the author, give out an address or phone number.

Any internet references contained in this work are current at publication time, but the publisher cannot guarantee that a specific location will continue to be maintained. Please refer to the publisher's website for links to authors' websites and other sources.

Llewellyn Publications
A Division of Llewellyn Worldwide Ltd.
2143 Wooddale Drive
Woodbury, MN 55125-2989
www.llewellyn.com

Printed in the United States of America

Other Books by Leeza Robertson

Animal Totem Tarot
Tarot Court Cards for Beginners
Tarot Reversals for Beginners
Pathworking the Tarot
Mermaid Tarot
Tarot Healer
The Divine Practice of Angel Numbers
Cirque du Tarot
Soul Cats Tarot
Tarot Priestess

Forthcoming Books by Leeza Robertson

The Book of Mermaid Magic (December 2022)
Angel Tarot
The Celestial Unicorn Tarot
Fairy Wheel Tarot
Legends of Avalon Tarot
Tarot Muse

CONTENTS

INTRODUCTION

Like all my works, *A Year of Angel Guidance* was heavily influenced by my Celtic/Roman heritage. It might seem an odd thing to admit, as this is a book about angels, but bear with me. I knew in my bones it was time to write about a new set of angels, one that has been ready and waiting for this new age to unfold. These angels knew that there would come a time when the ancestors would insist on us bringing our heads out of the clouds and planting our feet firmly on the ground. We only have so much "go big or go home" time before "home" starts to crumble through a lack of love, devotion, and attention. This book is about coming back to the little parts of life we overlook or take for granted and about finding the divine in the everyday, just like my Celtic/Roman ancestors did.

My ancestors—and possibly many of yours—lived in a time where it was completely normal to worship, pray to, and even set up altars for everyday deities. They would have a deity in their cupboard so that their pantries would always be fully stocked. My ancestors would give thanks each morning to deities of the fire for providing warmth, cooked food, and drinkable water. There was no aspect of my ancestor's lives that did not involve some form of honoring and expressing gratitude to the divine energy running through all things. And while this book isn't quite so micro-focused, the angels you will meet throughout in these pages work in a very similar fashion.

I wrote *A Year of Angel Guidance* not long after *Tarot Priestess*—although my editor hates it when I talk about a past work in a new work, I believe it is important in respect to how this book took shape. It was while doing research for that book that I dug deeply into the everyday practices of my ancestral line. I really wanted to understand how daily devotion had been taught through my personal lineage. My family never talked about its Roman roots much, even though my grandfather was a migrant who made his way to Australia in the late 1940s to escape war and poverty in Europe. He was one of the thousands who fled southern Italy and Sicily at the end of the Second World War. He died two weeks before my mother found out she was pregnant with me, meaning I never got to meet him. Just about everything I have learned about my Roman ancestors I have learned on my own. The most interesting was how many Celts populated the area in Sicily in which my grandfather was born. Celtic blood runs through both sides of my family tree. Their rituals have in many respects now become mine, and I have adapted some of them for what you will read here.

During my research time, the angels you are about to meet started to come to me. As if they were stepping forward through the mist, they presented themselves one by one. At first, I wasn't sure why they had sought me out or how our work together was meant to unfold. So as with most things "angel," I waited for them to tell me. Their message was clear: Some old ways needed to be new ways. I knew this was the daily devotion work I had just spent months researching. Because this is neither a book really about priesthood nor devotion, the angels and I had to figure out how to bring some old practices into a new age. The result is what you now hold in your hands.

How We Pulled It All Together

The angels were clear on wanting daily practices, small touchstones, and bite-sized pieces of guidance for every day of the year. It sounded easy at first, until we started putting all the content together. Then I started to notice how hard it is to actually do this work every single day. You see, I set myself the task of writing one message per day as if in conversation with the angels themselves. That worked for about ten weeks; then life happened, and it all went sideways.

I suspect the angels knew what was going to happen before we even began our journey together; me struggling to get the messages on the pages is just a larger metaphor for how we all struggle to get our daily practice in. Life is relentless. Stuff is happening all the time. Whether we admit it or not, chaos creeps into all our lives in one form or another, which is why the angels were so adamant we create something for every single day of the year. No matter what happens, you can always come back and start wherever you are.

This book is laid out to connect you with a new angel every single month. In that month you will work exclusively with your angel of the month and immerse yourself in the lessons, guidance, or messages they have set out for you. Because the messages have been co-created by myself and the angels, you will find that the daily messages sometimes sound like me and other times they come directly from the angels themselves. I did not wish to change this difference in voice even though it might seem weird from a reader's perspective. There were days when the angels felt it necessary to let you know they were right there with you, speaking to you directly from the page, not just through me but directly to you. It might seem strange to those of you who are new to channeled information, but you will get the hang of it.

Each month opens with a connection exercise in which you call forth the energy of the angel you will be working with, request their time and assistance, and connect them to your calendar. After that, you will move through the days of the week. Every month has a theme the angel has selected that offers the teachings for that theme, and every small piece of information you receive throughout the month is deliberately tuned to bring you into alignment with the energy of the theme and the angel walking alongside you for your monthly journey.

The month will end as it began—with prayer. At that time, you will perform a disconnection exercise to release the angel you have been working with, offer your thanks, and bring the monthly circle to an end. Just as it is important to open a circle, you need to make sure it is closed, too. Closing a circle stops energy from leaking into the next month and allows you to experience each month with renewed focus. In this way, you build upon the month before rather than dragging energy with you like shackles throughout the entire year. I have also included two check-in sections per month to keep you connected to your angel of the month and ensure you are still attuned to the frequencies of the monthly theme.

Altar Work

All energy needs a place to ground, a place where it can be honored, maintained, and held. Each month, you will build a space for your angel and the energy you will be working with. Think of that space as for your sacred work, where you will open, activate, check in, and close your journey each month. That space will be an altar, one you will build each month and then cleanse, clear, and rebuild until your full year with the angels is complete.

Altar work is the work of my ancestors; it is more than likely part of your ancestry as well. The Romans had altars everywhere … and I do mean everywhere—in their cupboards, on their tables, next to the hearths, beside their beds, at their front door, at their back door, and more! They were not always massive things with lots of candles or flowers, though those things did appear every so often. Mainly they contained drawings, paintings, or iconic carvings to the deity who ruled over the space in which they were placed. These days, you might see crosses or religious paintings or prints hanging in a Catholic house, especially over doorways.

In my Celtic heritage, bunches of flowers, seeds, and sometimes fruit were placed around the house to honor the deities of space. Songs would be sung to keep the energy of a deity around, or stories would be shared to honor a gathering. We still do this in so many ways; we just don't connect the dots to it being a ritualistic activity that we have carried in our blood—deep epigenetic memory from our ancestors. Religious or not, we are all ritualistic beings, which is why for so many people, altar work is like coming home.

Each month, you will be asked to set up an altar to the angel you will be working with. There are some suggestions in each chapter, but you can set up your altar in any way you choose. The angels would love for you to think of this altar work as a way of connecting to your own personal ancestry, to tap into the intuitive knowing that runs through you on how to create a sacred space just for your own personal work. You might consider having candles, pictures, salt for protection, dirt for grounding, crystals for different angels, and flowers as a symbol of growth.

Before you even start setting up your altar, take a moment to close your eyes; breathe slowly and deeply in through your nose and out through your mouth. Call whatever angel you will be working with for the month into your energy, and see if you can get a feel for what they would like upon their altar. Do they feel warm or cool? Is there a certain color that presents itself when they come close to you? What about images—do you see anything? Use your inner knowing and trust that whatever information you receive is correct. Even if you don't receive anything at all, it just means the angels will accept whatever altar you create for them. Now you are ready to move on to the next section and meet this new group of angels who are just so excited to work with you for the next year!

Meeting Your Angels

I used to wonder what it might be like to have an angel at my beck and call 365 days a year. Then it really happened. The year the angels came into my life and started to share their guidance with me changed me forever. Now it is my turn to pass it along to you. This book is a way of me paying forward many messages that transformed me, guidance that made me more present and grounded in my life, and not to mention information that opened my eyes to a world of angels I never knew existed—the realm of the guardians.

For the most part, people know of the archangels, as they tend to be in the spotlight. However, there is another set of angels, ones who get none of the fame but do most of the work in the human realm. In the pages that follow, I am happy to introduce to you the twelve angels who belong to a band of angels called your guardian angels. The guardians spend their entire existence working, walking, and living alongside humans. They are the unsung heroes of the angelic realm. You may not know their names just yet, but they are the ones who help you find that parking space close to the entrance. They are the ones who help you get all the green lights. They are also the ones who stop you, slow you down, and protect you.

You may have heard the term "guardian angel" before and may already have some predetermined ideas about what a guardian angel is. For our purposes here, the angels and I would like you to consider expanding upon that knowledge and opening yourself up to a slightly different approach. What you will learn may be very different from what you think you know. In fact, there is a very good chance you are going to learn about angels you have never heard of and experience messages and experiences you never knew these sorts of angels were capable of.

The twelve guardian angels you will work with are:

- Jana
- Bridgette
- Willow
- Faith
- Daniel
- Nel
- Penne
- Solis
- Sylvania
- Chana
- Sophia
- Lailah

Think of the angels as your invisible friends: they listen deeply when you speak and dream. They know the truth of your heart and want to help you pursue all your hopes and dreams. These angels want nothing more for you than for you to see how blessed you truly are, and they want to teach you how to make the world of material things a reflection of the beauty that lives inside you. They want to show you the path to freedom, joy, peace, and abundance—it is in your very makeup as a vibrational being made flesh. The ease or difficulty of the lessons, however, will depend on your level of resistance to seeing yourself the way the angels do.

In many ways, *A Year of Angel Guidance* is your daily dose of angelic medicine. For 365 days, you will have an angel in your corner. That angel will give you messages, guidance, and insights to help you navigate that which we call the human experience, a small balm for your soul. Sometimes your daily medicine will be active, requiring you to take action on a specific theme or idea for the day. Other times it might be more introspective and require you to go within or just observe how you navigate and negotiate your world.

The angels have made this even easier by dividing the book into twelve themes. Each month, your angelic medicine will be delivered around a certain theme, thirty to thirty-one bite-sized pieces of guidance for each theme. You will also start and close each month in ceremony with your angel, allowing you to create a devotional practice with your guardian angels. The practice will set the tone for the energy of the month to come. The twelve themes you will traverse over the next year are:

- Doorways
- Illumination
- Manifestation
- Growth
- Movement
- Transmutation
- Play
- Passion
- Transitions
- Gratitude
- Reflection
- Darkness

You might be wondering, "Why these angels and themes?" I am going to be incredibly transparent: As I was writing, the angels and themes shifted more than once. The angels wanted to make sure that the content, medicine, messages, and guidance were the best they could possibly bring forth. This book is very much written by them for you, dear reader. I am merely the vessel through which all of this came to pass. Sometimes that is an easy job, other times not so much. Think of these messages as being written in a partnership, the nonphysical energy we call the angels together with my physical self so that their words can be manifested into the realm of physical and material things.

Exercise: Making Space For Your New Guardians

It's not every day you need to find a way to make space for twelve angels. It might even seem a little overwhelming to those of your who have never undertaken a task like this. Inviting a new guide into your life can take time. You might feel vulnerable or apprehensive about letting them into your daily life, which is why we are going to do a very quick and simple connection exercise.

This will allow you to feel safe, steady, and stable as you allow each new guardian to make their way into your energy and life.

For this connection exercise, you will need:

- a white candle
- a window you can open
- a glass and a beverage of your choice

Begin by lighting your white candle. Now repeat the following:

> *Guardian angels, the light is on to guide your way.*

Next, open the window. You don't have to open it all the way; a crack will do. Now repeat the following:

> *Guardian angels, I have cleared the way for you to come through.*

To end your connection exercise, raise your glass. Now repeat:

> *Guardian angels, I raise a glass and make a toast to our new journey together.*

Now drink your beverage! And when you feel ready to disconnect, close the window. This will let your guardian angels know that you are ready for space and privacy. You can repeat this connection exercise whenever you want to bring your angels into your day.

Always remember that *you* get to decide when and how your relationship with the angels will take place. You are the one with free will and sovereignty, and you are the one who gets to set the rules of engagement.

User Guide to Your Messages

Let's talk about how to use the information you will find in the following chapters. The angels themselves have a few recommendations for how they would like you to use this content. This book is designed to be a yearlong journey that does not have to start on January 1 (though it would be amazing if it did). Each chapter is meant to be traveled from the start of the month to the end of the month. All the angels ask is that when you decide to embark on your journey, start at the very beginning of the month, no matter which month that may be. The angels and I understand that you have the free will to dive into any messages you want. You might even decide not to use them as we recommend it, and that is cool. We know you will get whatever you need from the text, regardless of how you decide to use the messages and the daily prompts. When we designed the content for each of the chapters, however, we did it to flow in a sequential manner.

Some people are crazy about numbers and special dates. We get that you will be tempted to flip to your birthday and look at that message. You may even explore the theme of the month you were born in—by all means, feel free. You can search dates for anniversaries and any other special occasions on your personal calendar. Be advised that the content works best when the monthly messages are done in order. Play with the content and have fun. Don't allow your resistance to stop you from having an immersive experience with the angels.

Before Moving On

Let's talk a little about the wording and language you will see in the following pages, as it is a channeled text. You'll notice the use of "we," which for the most part indicates the angels and myself. When I am streaming incoming messages, the feeling is "we," not "them" and "myself." The energy and consciousness feel like one combined stream. Another word you will encounter frequently is the "mundane." Many people don't like this word—we don't like to think of ourselves or our lives as boring. However, the angels don't see it that way. To them, the "mundane" is the everyday, the world of repetition, lessons, and consequences. It is the world we humans live in. What is interesting about the word "mundane" is that, whereas we see that word and think *boring*, the angels see that word and think *magical*. Perception really is everything. The angels and I challenge you to start seeing the word "mundane" as a form of magic, a portal to miracles. That sounds a lot more fun, doesn't it?

In many respects, *A Year of Angel Guidance* is a snippet of my daily life. The angels first entered my life in 2009 and have been offering up their little angelic doses ever since. That said, I don't take it every day. We humans have free will, and part of that free will is the ability to refuse angelic assistance. I have said "no thanks" plenty of times. To some, that might seem stupid. The thing is, though, making mistakes is part of the human journey, shaping us in many ways. Not all mistakes will hurt us or cause us pain; in fact, some might make us laugh or bring new friends into our lives who end up creating magic.

Remember that you do not have to take the angels' guidance every single day. Maybe a bit of guidance doesn't resonate with you at a particular moment—that is perfectly fine. You will not be punished in any way, shape, or form, nor will you make the angels angry. I am not even sure it's possible to piss them off; if it was, I am pretty sure I would have done it already. The angels are not people, so they do not have our same emotions or even physical bodies. They are just a band of loving energy that offers help when we want it, which means that they can't be offended or upset. The only one with the capacity for serious feelings is you.

This seems like a fabulous place to finish up this introduction and allow you to start your journey. Now that you know what you are getting into, who you are going on this journey with, and what some of the rules of engagement are, you can now walk the path. All I can say is enjoy the ride: remember this is your journey and your year—you get to do it on your terms. The angels are here as guides (and they are pretty good at it), and this particular group was made to guide you. Now it's up to you to listen. So, buckle up and let the excitement begin!

Chapter One
THE
REALM OF
THE GUARDIANS

All meetings start in the same place: with an introduction. Seeing as this book is your meet-and-greet with these twelve new angels, we should spend a bit of time introducing each of them and giving you the opportunity to get to know them a little better before diving into working with them for the next year. But before we do just that, let's talk a little bit about the realm of guardians. Oftentimes when I am asked about the archangels, I describe them as the band of angels that pushes us to raise our awareness, expand our vibrational energy, and constantly uplevel our beliefs, thoughts, and feelings. In many respects, the archangels belong to ascension energy. The guardians are very different, as they are grounded, practical, and more interested in assisting us in navigating the muck of human experience.

Say you want to bring more love into your life. The archangels would like us to think about love as energy; they would want us to become one with love's vibrational energy and embody it rather than look for it in the external world. The guardians, however, want to help you find love in the material world. They would give you practical assistance, steps, and instructions for attracting a romantic partner into your life. Do you see the difference? Theory vs Practice. That is one of the key differences between these two bands of angels. There are others, but for the scope of this book, that is pretty much all you need to know. So make a cuppa, get comfy, and let me introduce your new guardian angels.

Jana: Guardian Angel of Doorways

When Jana first appeared to me, which was very early on a chilly February morning, she (and yes, this angel did present herself as female) introduced herself by saying "Hi. My name is Jana, and I am your guardian angel of the door." I just stared at her through my yet-to-be-caffeinated eyeballs and replied, "Huh?" She went on to further explain, to which I replied "Oh, are *you* the reason I can never remember why I entered a room?" She rolled her eyes hard. I took that as a no; apparently those were not the sort of doorway she was referring to. Jana is the guardian angel of opportunity portals, things we humans tend to refer to as doorways. Think of the expression "when one door closes, another opens"— that's Jana. She watches over the opening and closing of doors as well as making some doors visible and others invisible. I must admit that I think she is more of a superhero than an angel. I mean, what a cool job!

We humans are always finishing and beginning new cycles. We finish something and the door closes; we start something else and another door opens. Jana explained that because every being in the universe is in a constant state of beginnings and endings, many doors are always appearing and disappearing. Jana is one of the few angels that deals with us humans. She also explained that she loves the saying "opportunity knocks," as she feels it explains what she does well. When your intent and your path merge a doorway, sometimes a selection of doorways appear but you can only go through one of them—the one that your guardian angel knocks on. Jana explained that for the most part, we don't hear the knock with our ears; instead it is a knowing or a pull or tug in the direction our guardian angel feels is the next right step for us.

Jana also pointed out that we don't always walk through the door we are pulled toward. There can be lots and lots of different reasons why we may ignore the angel's knock, the biggest being fear, as we aren't so great with the unknown. The angels are okay if we ignore them; they totally understand, and Jana said she is often on standby to offer a door again when the time feels more aligned. She told me an opportunity never goes away—it just waits until the conditions line up again, but she also added not to worry if they do not. There are always plenty of other doors and opportunities. I asked her if she thought now was a good time to be introduced formally to the world at large. Her answer: "The conditions were aligned and the door appeared, so here I am, knock knock." Oh yeah, even angels think they are funny.

Bridgette: Guardian Angel of Illumination

Confession time: When I first met this particular angel, I thought she was a goddess. She has so many similarities to the goddess of a similar name: she is connected to elemental fire, she deals with light, and she seems to prefer working in the darker months of the year. However, Bridgette was very clear that she is *not* the goddess Brigit and has always been a guardian angel walking right alongside us as we evolve and continue to grow as a species. Bridgette loves showing humans their inner light, the spark the angels see but we often doubt. She told me how much joy she gets when one of her humans finally realizes how brightly they can shine.

This angel seriously loves her job. In fact, out of all the angels you will meet, I believe in my heart that Bridgette gets the most fulfillment out of her work. It's not that the others don't enjoy what they do; it's more like meeting someone who was just *made* to do something. Bridgette's energy is one of the first things you will notice when she is around. It is infectious and makes the air sizzle with anticipation for what will come. You might even find yourself warming up from the inside as your inner light flickers on in response to this angel's presence. If someone tells you that you made their day or brought light to their life, your guardian angel Bridgette will not be far away.

Just like the seasons, we all go through light moments in our lives followed by darker ones. Our experience as physical beings wasn't meant to only have one setting. During these stormier times, Bridgette will be closest. She might work through you to assist someone else, or she might be there to help light the path through your dark-night-of-the-soul moment. Wherever illumination is needed, she will be there, ready to assist in whatever way she is required. Like all the guardians, she cannot and will not ever push light onto you if you are not ready for it. She works hand in hand with another guardian you will meet, together balancing the light and dark, as both states are sacred. When you are ready, all you have to do is ask and Bridgette will be there, armed with a lantern and ready to show you how to shine once again.

Willow: Guardian Angel of Manifestation

There have been many times when I have thought manifestation is overhyped, that it went from being about a simple energetic process to a get-rich-quick scheme. People got very hooked on getting stuff and lost sight of how manifestation energy can enhance life in real, lasting ways. Guardian Willow came to me in one of those cynical moments in 2013. At the time, I had just landed my very first publishing contract and was wanting a way to make sure it wasn't my last, but the manifestation teachings at the time had strayed into yachts, luxury cars, and finding a rich husband—none of which had absolutely any appeal to me. I struggled with manifesting for a long time. As it is often taught, manifestation can be super stressful for people with anxiety; it is almost impossible for the anxious mind to trick itself into thinking something is there that clearly isn't. If that was the case, anxiety wouldn't be an issue.

Willow showed me multiple paths to manifesting energy, ones that did not trigger my anxiety, ones that allowed me to feel more like I was working toward a plan and less wishful thinking. She also showed me the difference between having an optimistic attitude and toxic positivity. Willow taught me that manifestation is not a one-size-fits-all energy. It works differently for different people, and her job is to guide us along the path that works best for us as individuals. Through working with Willow, I learned how to tap in and leverage my own personal manifestation energy. We hope that after you spend some time with her, you will too. Her energy feels like a gentle nudge, a reassuring presence when self-doubt raises its head. Willow will poke you a little each day to follow the energetic threads to things you heart truly desires, creating momentum.

In many respects guardians Willow, Faith, and Daniel work hand in hand. Their energy is very similar, and they all play very key roles in moving us along the path of creation/manifestation/inspiration, which is one more thing Willow taught me. Manifestation is a team sport, not an individual pursuit. The more we try to do it alone, the more frustrating it will become. Willow sometimes presents herself as an opportunity, a clear path to what was once blocked. She can also be an open door where there wasn't even a door before. She will show you that the magic is really in the everyday small tasks you take for granted. Willow is the master of mundane magic, that is, things you consider boring and regular. If there is one thing I have learned from working with Willow over the years, it is that nothing—and I mean *nothing*—is without magic. The very thing you need might be right under your nose, so don't overlook it in favor of focusing on fancy clothes and even fancier dreams. Of course, there's nothing wrong with wanting nice things; Willow is more than happy to help you manifest your millions. More importantly, she wants you to learn how to manage and maintain that energy so you can see that the millions you dream of might actually have been right in front of your face this whole time.

Faith: Guardian Angel of Growth

I would like to tell you I met this angel while walking in an ancient woodland or hiking a pilgrimage trail, but no such thing happened. In fact, I first met Faith more than ten years ago while standing in front of a dead houseplant. Like many people who claim they have no green thumbs, I have killed many houseplants over the years. (Succulents are my nemesis to this day.) As I lamented yet another plant I had failed to keep alive, Faith appeared. She was decked out in full gardening gear, which seemed over the top considering we were inside. But that's Faith, ever the ray of sunshine on a stormy day. She wasn't alone, either—it appeared that she had brought some faerie friends with her. Wherever Faith is, you can be assured fae magic is nearby.

Guardian Faith embodies an energy we all talk about yet few of us know how to really use. Growing a life, growing as a human, and growing our soul are not easy tasks. We make mistakes and end up with a collection of dead houseplants along the way, metaphorically speaking. Growth requires a very systematic process, one that has plenty of room for flexibility and exploration but that also requires you to travel through every step one at a time. That last part, "one at a time," is one that we in our modernized, fast-moving society tend to screw up. Our world seems to spin on the axis of capitalistic pursuits; in it there is no time, energy, and too many dead houseplants. We carry around devices that give us instant access to almost anything and allows others to have constant access to us. The whole idea of slowing down and focusing on a plan, process, or system is just not keeping pace with the world of Instagram influencers and TikTokers, both of which may not exist in five years' time.

Most people call to Faith when life slaps them in the face—only in those times do most people start thinking about growing, creating, sustaining, and maintaining. Faith wants to remind you that you don't have to wait *until* life gets bad to slip into her energy. She is always available, and I am not sure she ever takes off her gardening gear. Faith wants to show you how to follow the natural energy in your cells, soul, and planet. She wants to help you shift away from the fast track and onto the life track. This doesn't mean you won't have any more dead houseplants, like the dead tree staring me down in the corner of my office. But it does mean you will have a better understanding of why some things go from seed to sapling to blooming plant and others do not. Faith will show you another path to fulfillment, one that is not about stuff and status but about trust, confidence, and harmony. Faith, myself, and the fae all hope you find your flow in the pages of her chapter. We hope you take time to follow the steps and allow yourself to sink into the satisfaction of becoming a grower, not a collector.

Daniel: Guardian Angel of Movement

I met Daniel in a year where I felt stuck, not only in my life like nothing was happening and there was nowhere to go, but also when I had a frozen shoulder—my physical body was literally stuck! The year was 2018, and I was just coming off a year that felt heavy, blocked, and stagnant. In my mind, I was feeling as though I had little control in getting things moving again. My internal stress was so bad that it froze my shoulder into place; my left arm became totally useless. I could not use it to wash myself, and getting dressed was incredibly hard. Life in general became very difficult. I don't like difficulty, nor am I someone who likes to feel limited, so I set about researching how to undo the damage to my body and spirit. Enter the guardian Daniel.

Through Daniel, I was able to get my arm and mind working correctly again in about sixty days. It wasn't easy, and learning to focus on movement and keeping things moving was a complete shift for me. For the most part, movement comes naturally to young people. As we age, however, we tend to become a little more still and find more excuses not to move, not only regarding physical activity but also including things such as jobs, relationships, where we live, travel, and more. It was through Daniel I learned how all those pieces came together, how when one part of life grinds to a halt, the rest of the pieces can only self-sustain for so long before they start slowing down. The same is true for when things start to pick up and gain momentum. Ever since Daniel has been in my life, I have been very mindful about movement and making sure I am constantly keeping momentum going in my life.

Daniel appears to those who are ready for a change: movement means things won't stay as they are currently. Movement shifts things around, and people and places tend to move with this new energy. Though as Daniel always reminds me, major shifts take a lot of concentrated movement to create. For our purposes here, you probably won't see life-altering moves, unless of course you want them. Nevertheless, it is a good idea to set an intention at the beginning of Daniel's chapter. Let him know in exactly what areas of your life you are seeking movement. Use the daily prompts and lessons to keep consistent movement energy flowing through that intended area. And allow Daniel to show you where else this energy could be channeled. You will know when your guardian angel of movement is around: life won't feel so hard. Your mind won't feel so bogged down, and your body will want to get up and move. Energy is meant to move and we are pure energy. Luckily for us, we have such an incredible guardian in Daniel to make sure we stay moving.

Nel: Guardian Angel of Transmutation

Of all the lessons in this book, this was the one I personally struggled with the most. It wasn't that I did not understand the mission—it was the fact that undergoing the transmutation process requires total and utter surrender. Guardian Nel's job is to help us let go and hand our control and power over to what cannot be recognize mentally, physically, or with our senses. I also think Nelys, who prefers to be called Nel, has a much harder job than some of the other guardians; it's not like humans have *ever* been known to be pig-headed and stubborn. In reality, we are transmuting or changing all the time, shifting from one phase of our lives to another, transforming from one way of being and doing to another. Nel points out that this sort of change is often undetectable to the ego mind, meaning we are less resistant to it and move more easily through the stages. The trouble happens when we mentally process change, which allows the ego mind to start calculating risks and benefits. That analysis in turn usually leads to us digging in our heels, such that we end up having to be dragged through the transmutation process.

This resistance to what is a very natural process is at the core of a lot of human suffering, or so the guardians say. I am somewhat of a poster child for this suffering: I suffer from acute stress, and my worry meter is often through the roof. Nel is one of the angels who helps me navigate stress, reminding me that change is normal and worrying about things I cannot change or control stops me from getting in the flow of creation. And now this guardian is at your disposal as well, though technically she always has been. Now having this awareness means you have some assistance. Although you will learn more about the subtle differences between change, transformation, and the act of transmutation in Nel's chapter, let us say for now that the reason humans tend to resist transmutation is because it changes us so deeply and profoundly. In other words, it is bigger than a normal change—it is long-lasting and has ripple effects in all parts of our lives. In tarot, we might call it a Tower moment.

Nel is used to being around energy that resists her presence. Her energy is loving, kind, and very compassionate, very similar to that of archangel Jophiel. In fact, the first time I came in contact with Nel, I thought it was Jophiel. The only difference I noticed was that the energy seemed less bouncy. Jophiel reminds me of a loving heart with ADHD. Her energy is off the walls sometimes. Nel is calm, quiet, soft-spoken, and gentle-footed. There is nothing harsh or jarring about her, which also makes her easy to overlook. However, you cannot deny how you feel when this guardian is around—you feel supported, as if someone has you wrapped in a giant pair of wings. You might even feel loved in a way you have never felt before. Nel is the midwife of change. She holds space for us to evolve, move through our karmic cycles, and shapeshift into whatever creation we choose to be. Change is the only constant our world, and I, for one, am thankful to know that Nel is here to hold our hand, rub little calming circles over our backs, and reassure us that we are all going to be okay.

Penne: Guardian Angel of Play

Penne, or Pen as this guardian likes to be called, is with us from birth. Because self-expression is part of the energy Pen comes to teach us, this angel can appear to each of us differently. You can refer to angel Penne using her/she/his/he/them/they. To me, Pen predominantly appears in female form, so I often call this angel Pen and use her/she pronouns. Who we are, how we see the world, and how we choose to move through it is part of the energy Pen teaches us. She does not really understand when or how we became so rigid in our physical forms. She believes if we were never meant to experience what it means to shapeshift, we would never have invented games like dress-up or professional acting—she is a huge fan of both.

Play, according to Pen, is meant to teach us how to relax, explore, ignite our imaginations, and deepen our senses of adventure. In turn, these activities make us excellent problem-solvers and allow us to be more adaptable in our ever-changing lives. Guardian Penne can take anything and turn it into play—and I do mean *anything*. She has helped me play my way out of an anxiety attack and acute stress, and she has most recently helped me play my way out of a very horrible professional breakup. What I have learned through working with Pen over the years is that play and the energy it moves through our body shifts our way of thinking. When we change the way we think, we change the way we act. Play can therefore be incredibly healing to the body, mind, and emotions. The moment we slip into the energy of play, we coat our nervous system in a cooling balm that calms it down and brings us back to center—yes, it's that powerful. You will know when Pen is around when your body will start to sway, and you might even feel like dancing. You'll get a glint in your eye and suddenly mischief is on your mind.

As you will learn in Penne's chapter, play isn't just about games. There is much more to the energy than perhaps you have been taught. You will find multiple ways to play and use play's energy to shift into its more healing and calming vibrational forms. Pen and I also hope working with the energy of play for a whole month might inspire you to do something new and different. I know she has been working her magic on me the whole time we have been working on this book; she has helped me with all the revisions and edits as a form of play. She keeps me busy so stress and anxiety won't overwhelm me.

We live in a world that is always on high alert. Our nervous systems have been through a lot over the course of human history, making play needed now more than ever. This is the time to take Penne by the hand and let her guide you to places that are more healing and calming. Let her guide you to work more with the natural rhythm of your inspired soul self. All you have to do is move through the lessons in her chapter and let the magic unfold.

Solis: Guardian Angel of Passion

I first met this angel in 2010 through my wife at a work event. My wife has twin guardian angels, Solomon and Solis, the latter of whom stepped forward and asked to be a part of this book. Seeing as he had been a part of our household for so long, it seemed the polite thing to do. Through Solis, I learned more about passion than in anything I'd read. Between 2012 and 2014, there was a popular movement called the Passion Project. Although I knew a few people who were part of it, the way they spoke about passion didn't resonate with me. The project isn't really around anymore, so I suppose it stopped resonating with others as well. For me it felt like a hopeless pursuit and something outside of the way I personally move through the world.

Unlike my wife, who is a very sensitive and emotional flower, I am super cerebral; I tend to intellectualize my emotions instead of wearing them. The whole "passion" thing seemed to be about finding your passion flag, turning it into a power suit, and then singing about passion from the rooftops. That is *so* not me, and I was sure I was never going to find my passion or figure out what it meant for people like me. It was through Solis that I learned that passion is an energy that shifts, moves, bends, changes, and flows. It is not one single thing, nor is it static and immovable. Most importantly, he taught me that although passion isn't going to look the same for everyone, you should be able to feel similarities. Switching from thinking about passion as an energy—rather than an attachment to a thing or person—changed my world forever. Who knows, maybe it will change yours as well.

You will know when Solis is around, as his energy feels like spring sun on a late winter day. It is just the right sort of warmth that brings a sudden smile to your face, the type of sunlight that allows you to drop your shoulders, take a deep breath, and feel like all's right with the world. Solis calls this his passion-for-life breath. Things tend to flow much easier when Solis is around, and time seems to speed up because you are enjoying yourself so much. Passion is one of those energies that sneaks up on you and before you know it, you have lost hours because you were so focused on what you were doing that the whole world just faded away. These are the moments where Solis burns the brightest, in the flow of your personal joy, whatever that might be for you. Passion is also very unique to the individual—what lights the fires of passion energy in one person won't be the same for another, but we can all be thankful that guardian angel Solis is here to assist us.

Sylvania: Guardian Angel of Transitions

Because I believe in transparency, I need to admit that this guardian is new to me. Sylvania came to me about six months before I began mapping out this book. At the time, I was working my buns off with a business that doesn't exist anymore and wrapping up a couple of deck and book projects. My time, energy, and mind were stretched beyond capacity, and I was worried I was not going to keep all my commitments. This was when Sylvania stepped in and showed me the path to the magical part of the daily routine known as transition. I knew about the concept but had not been very good at putting it into practice in my daily life. Luckily for me, Sylvania was there. I truly believe that if I had stuck to this angel's protocols, I would not have burned out at the end of 2021. That's how important Sylvania's lessons are.

This particular guardian is not really an organizer, nor would I call them efficient in any other aspect except for their own. But when it comes to transitions, space, and all the little micro-gaps in our day and life, this guardian is an expert magic-maker. Believe it or not, we have a lot of time in the day in which we allow our energy to leak out, our minds to stray, and our body to freeze. For the most part, we do not notice this happening at all because we aren't taught about transitions. I personally learned about them from Brendon Burchard through the Growth Day app, an app for entrepreneurs that helps them, well, grow. Sylvania and I decided that if transitions were important for entrepreneurs to learn, they were doubly important for everyone else—because it is in dealing with small everyday tasks that we usually experience burnout.

It is important to point out here that Sylvania is not just a magical guardian for the extremely busy. They are an everyday angel whose purpose is to assist us through our day-to-day goings-on, even if we aren't overworked. There is no entry point in asking for this guardian's help or assistance. We all go through multiple transitions in our life, which will be explored in the pages of Sylvania's chapter. Everyone will need this angel's assistance at some point, if not right now, though the angels and I are confident that once you have worked with transitions for a full month, your mind will be blown when you understand how important they actually are. You will notice when Sylvania is around because there will be a flutter of energy in between tasks, a feeling like a butterfly wing beating on your hand when seasons are about to change, a tickling sensation when the traffic is about to change, or a whisper to get up and walk around when you have finished one task at your computer. This guardian is about letting you know a space or gap has appeared and it is time to use it to clear, reset, and restore. After working with Sylvania, you will never look at your daily tasks the same way.

Chana: Guardian Angel of Gratitude

Apparently I met this particular guardian when I was in Greece. I don't remember it, but that's what Chana has told me. That trip was not a pleasant one; I spent it with my head in a toilet bowl because people kept slipping meat into my dishes even when I asked them not to. It was three weeks from hell, and I won't ever be going back to Greece ever again. However, it was on that trip where Chana first came to me to remind me of why I was there and how grateful I would be once the ordeal was over with (which I was). Gratitude is a lot weirder than people think; it shows up in some of the strangest moments in our lives. Most people believe it is something we do with a journal in which we list things we are thankful for. It can certainly be that, but there are also many times when it is so far removed from that experience that we don't even notice it. That was me in Greece circa 2006.

Chana reminds us that most people approach gratitude as something in hindsight, when we look back and see worse things that could have been. Then there is the journaling list, in which, again, some items are from the past. Chana taught me that the best way to tap into gratitude's energy is through being thankful for things we do not have yet, to "thank it forward." Out of all the ways Chana has taught me to be grateful over the years, thanking it forward is my personal favorite. When I started going deeper with the energy of gratitude, I bought a silver pot that sits on my main altar. Inside it are rolled up and folded notes, and the occasional sticky note with things I am grateful for. Some are past energy, some are present energy, and some are future energy. Ultimately they will all become past energy, which is why gratitude is mostly hindsight. The point of using the silver pot is to remind me to put things in it and see this form of being thankful as devotion, another thing Chana taught me that helped me deepen my gratitude practice. Giving thanks means more than listing things; it also means diving deeper into the "why" and "how" of gratitude energy: Why am I grateful for this thing/person/situation/opportunity and how will it enhance my daily life? You will know Chana is near when you feel the need to expand and explore your gratitude, feeling more than surface-level thankful, feeling something deep in your heart. You can feel this type of gratitude throughout your whole nervous system, radiating through your electromagnetic field, lighting you up and making you a gratitude beacon. Chana loves turning on the light inside a person and powering that light with the energy of gratitude. The next time someone says you are glowing, know that there is a good chance that Chana may be around.

Sophia: Guardian of Reflection

Most of our lives are reflected to us in either our broken shards or worst moments, or the celebratory cups of our finest moments. We catch moments of ourselves frozen in time, beamed back to us for further introspection. Reflections are just that: moments in time reaching out to us to take another look. Like a clue in a mystery novel, there is something in that moment that is important to where you are right now. Your soothing guardian Sophia is here to help you dive deep into the great mystery of yourself and assist you in finding the answers and solutions you require. She will also teach you that not all reflections deal with the past—some might even show you how to look into what is coming so you can prepare accordingly. I must admit when I first sat down with Sophia to work on her chapter, I had no idea how complex reflections really were. I had some work with this guardian before but it was nothing like what is mapped out in her chapter. You are in for a master class on reflections.

I have been trying to pinpoint exactly when guardian Sophia entered my life, but I feel like she has always been there, even before I knew who she was. I don't want to say she was lurking, though to be fair, my feeling is that the angels often lurk, hoping we will notice them and ask them to do something. But even as someone who has spent a lot of their lives with their nose in a research book, I know Sophia has been with me. She loves wisdom, knowledge, and understanding, which are all, according to her, the gifts reflection gives. If Sophia is around, you will notice the following clues: you experience a moment of clarity that clears up a problem or receive a flash of inspiration that feels as though it has been echoed from across the ages. Sophia loves to point you toward books, websites, and even real life classes. Wherever there is a space and place for reflection, Sophia will be there. She could be your "a-ha!" moment on a stormy day.

Now I know there might be those among you who think spending the whole month dealing with the topic of reflections is a little tedious or banal, so let me put it another way: the chapter on reflections is very much a month-long deep dive into discovery of you and your past, present, and future. All told, it makes a month seem a bit short. Sophia will guide you through every day so you can follow the clues, look for the signs, and know when and where you are dealing with different points on your own personal timeline. I know that I personally could spend a year working through reflections and still want more (but then I'm a giant nerd). Prepare to buy some new books, take some new classes, and have your journal and a pen ready—Sophia would love for you to take notes. Maybe do some wrist-loosening exercises before you start this one—see you on the other side of the looking glass.

Lailah: Guardian of Darkness

We all spend time in the dark; darkness is a natural state of our existence. Without it, we would have no understanding of light. To say that darkness is only the absence of light wildly misunderstands the healing and transformative properties darkness holds. We all come from the dark, and in many respects it creates us—it gives us a protected space to grow, expand, and gain consciousness. It is within this sacred space of burgeoning life that you will find guardian Lailah, whose job is to guide us through our time in the dark.

We all respond differently in the dark. Not one of us has the exact same experience in the quiet, secure space darkness creates for us. Lailah knows this well and is able to make sure each of us is attended to in the way we require and need. That said, you might find it interesting that you probably won't have your initial meeting with this guardian in the dark—instead, you will meet her in the light, on a bright sunny day where everything around seems perfect and complete. It's the day before all hell breaks loose in your life. I know this information makes her sound more like some sort of harbinger than a guardian, but bear with me.

For the most part, we are not good at sustaining happiness. So many of us believe that joy and happiness are capped, limited, and there is only so much that can go around. So when we have a day or even a couple of days that seem too good to be true, our ego minds get fearful and stir up trouble. That trouble can manifest in arguing with our spouse, co-worker, or friend. We could even feel guilty for experiencing such happiness and joy. Or—my personal favorite and the one that usually triggers Lailah to show up in my life—we become very suspicious about all the good in our life and start actively looking for places where things will go wrong. These games our ego minds play are often called sabotage triggers. When we are in the midst of one, the guardian of darkness will be there to help us navigate the swirling emotions that have come to rain on our happiness parade.

When we're feeling fearful that the good times won't last is not the only time Lailah can show up in our lives. Having worked with this guardian for a long time now, I know firsthand that she is also a wonderful healer and will open the darkness for you to rest, restore, and reset. In this respect she is an introvert's best friend: she loves crawling into a pillow fort with a good book and blocking out the noise of the world. Because the dark is complex and doesn't have a one-size-fits-all energy to it, you will learn more about darkness in Lailah's chapter then you ever have before. Even I learned some new tricks. No matter what your current relationship with the dark is, Lailah will be there to hold your hand, steady you, and show you everything you need to learn or heal when you set foot in her domain. Her energy is like a warm hug, a soft tender energy that makes you suddenly feel safe and secure. I like to think of the feeling she brings as a warm jam doughnut that has just been rolled in sugar and cinnamon. She brings a pillowy soft place to land, wrapped in a blanket of darkness, sprinkled with hope, love, and boundless possibilities.

Now that you've met the crew and learned more about who they are, what they do, and where in your life they might be floating around. Next, it's time to turn this page and start your own personal journey. Start wherever you are, in whichever month and day it is, flip to that spot, and let your year of magic and miracles begin.

Chapter Two
JANUARY

Jana
The Angel of Doorways

A new year, a new list of possibilities awaits you. Your angel of the month will help you close the door on the year you've just left behind and assist you in finding the door for the year to come. With so many options to consider, your angel of doorways is perfect to have at your side as you decide what you would most like to experience in the year ahead. Throughout this month, your angel is going to give you lessons, messages, and guidance around doorways that could take the form of instructional tasks to ground the lesson. You will sometimes use meditation, observation, or receive guidance that may be more abstract, as the material is channeled. Just know that whatever you personally receive from the daily prompt is correct and valid. Jana asks that you think about how you want to feel this coming cycle: What feelings do you wish to engage in as you move from one month to the next? She wants you to understand that knowing how you want to feel allows you to make more efficient decisions over the coming year. If you want to feel more kindness, make an effort to place yourself in more experiences filled with kindness. If you wish to feel more love, make more loving decisions. Jana says it is easier to find a door when you know how it would feel to walk through it.

Connection Prayer: Bringing in the
Energy of the Angel of Doorways

To get the most out of your month with Jana, set up your January altar as described in the introduction. Remember to include two pictures on your altar: one of an open doorway, and one of a closed doorway for this month. These pictures symbolize what you are saying goodbye to and what you are greeting and welcoming in. They also represent the doors you are closing from the previous year and the doors you are opening for the coming year. A white candle is best for your January altar, as it is the color of potential and pure possibility. I also recommend leaving space on your altar to add things to it as you move through your month. Once you have your altar cleansed and set up, light your candle and say the following prayer to bring in the energy of Jana and connect her to your January:

> *Angel of Doorways, I summon thee;*
> *Assist me in opening the doors of the new year,*
> *While allowing me to close the doors*
> *Of the year I have just left behind.*
> *Angel Jana, walk with me;*
> *Show me which doors will expand me.*
> *Guide me to the doors*
> *That will bring me joy,*
> *That will bring me love,*
> *That will bring me health,*
> *That will bring me wealth.*
> *Walk with me as I navigate this month;*
> *Whisper in my ear.*
> *Teach me new ways of beginning;*
> *Open my heart and let your light in.*
> *Angel of Doorways, I surrender to your wisdom*
> *In body, mind, and spirit.*

Once you are done with your connection prayer, you can leave your candle to burn out if it is safe to do so. If not, blow the candle out and make sure you say something along the lines of: "I now blow this candle out in the knowledge that my prayer has been heard," before extinguishing the flame. Adding this statement closes your ritual and seals the sacred circle of your prayer.

Messages for the Days of the Month

January 1

In order for something to truly begin, something else must truly end. Close the door on what is now done and complete. Lock it and throw away the key. There is no going back, only moving forward. Before you turn away from the closed door of the past, thank it. Be grateful for what it has taught you and honor those lessons. They have bought you to this new threshold and allowed you to make new choices, so what will those new choices be? What new journey would you like to begin? The possibilities may be endless, but there is only so much you can experience at any given time. For now, just start with one. Start with one thing that feels good, feels aligned, and is in the flow of the new energy you want to build upon with each passing day. New beginnings don't only start at the beginning of the year; they can start at the beginning of every single day. That means you have 365 new beginnings, 365 possibilities to explore—and it all starts today.

January 2

Not all journeys are meant to be taken alone. There are times when it is essential to have a trusted companion by your side: a loved one, a pet, or even one of your angels. Just know that today, two heads are better than one. There is another point of view you need to see, as well as another possible path you may not yet be aware of. Everything around you is both new and old. You are shutting one door and opening another, so you want to make sure the door you open does not lead you right back to from where you just came. This happens when we aren't paying attention and just gravitate to what has a feeling of familiarity or comfort. Having a friend by your side may provide the awareness you need in order to stop repeating the mistakes of the past. Use the buddy system today, and find a friend to share your journey with.

January 3

Today is for celebrating small wins around your new year. Take a look around and start listing all the new things in your life you wish to celebrate. Have you made a new friend or acquired new housing? Maybe you just want to celebrate a new you in a new year, bursting with new ideas, beliefs, and excitement. No matter what it is, the energy of celebration surrounds you today. So, raise a glass (it can even be water, coffee, or tea) and say cheers! Use these small wins as a way to start building your success vortex for the year. See each win you celebrate today as a seed you are planting in your yearlong garden of joy, happiness, and abundance. Plant these seeds now and continue to give them energy throughout the year. Before you know it, you will have a garden full of blessings at harvest time. And remember: what you do today is what you will live tomorrow.

January 4

All new things need a reason to be; they need a structure and a plan or, at the very least, an intention for their creation. As you move into a new year, it is time to think about what things are going to show up this year. What plans, goals, dreams do you have for the coming year, and how do you plan on making sure they happen? Today is about creating your map, charting your course, and setting the stage for the fun you wish to have. Although it is good to have as much detail as possible when setting out on a new adventure, just remember to leave space for the angels to create magic and miracles. Once you have your plan and read it over a couple of times, you will set creation energy into motion. Things will start to move and shift, and the threads of your desires will want to manifest in the most divine way, so make sure you leave enough space for it to happen. You will start to see things show up when, where and how they are the most aligned to you, your goals, and the miracles designed for you.

January 5

Not only is this a new year, it is a new month and a new day. It is another opportunity to try something you haven't tried before, sometimes in the spur of the moment, other times with planning for creating different experiences.

Planning means sitting down and really thinking about things you have never done and making a list. There will be things you wanted to do but didn't and things you never considered doing but would like to explore. Change doesn't have to show up out of the blue; you can plan for it and deliberately create it. Today is one of those planning days. Once you have your list, find three things that really speak to your heart and soul and put them on your calendar to do over the next month or two. The angels love change, as it creates expansion energy in the universe. Just by making this list and committing to follow through with something different this year, you have helped the angels grow the universe—yay, you!

January 6

You pass through many doorways in your home without even thinking about it, moving from one space to another, one environment to another. As you move into this new year, it is worth taking a moment to see if you want to be more strategic about the many different experiences in your own home. Consider how you wish to feel as you move from one room to the next. Imagine each room creating a feeling of love, joy, and abundance. Angel Jana wants you to remember that these experiences you wish to create start in your mind first and then in your home. Your home is a mini-version of the larger world you want to play in. She asks, "Does your home reflect this desire?" If not, it is time to begin creating a new world right inside your home, using the doorways as portals to new possibilities within each room you visit.

January 7

Before you move too far into the new year, it is important to take stock of the lessons you have learned from the previous year. You do not have to keep repeating the same lesson over and over again; repetition happens when one does not take stock and acknowledge what has been learned, or see what new possibilities have now opened up. Today, list everything you learned in the previous year and identify what new energy this lesson has brought into your life. If you wish to bring any of this new energy into this new year, state it in your list. Whatever you do not wish to bring with you, give thanks to it by writing the words, "Thank you, I release you," across the lesson. This simple yet intentional act will raise your awareness to what feels like repeating energy and what is filled to the brim with new exciting potential.

January 8

At the beginning of every year, it is important to take stock of what you have. It might seem like a boring and mundane task, but the angels know that when one cannot see their bounty, listing it out loud instantly moves the person into an energy of abundance. Jana also knows this simple task, which will be repeated throughout the year, will stop you from being attracted to the doorway of lack. So what do you have? What resources do you currently have at your disposal, and how are you going to use them to your benefit? Keep in mind that this is not just about money; it is about all your material resources. If you have a garden or outdoor space for pots and plants, that's a resource for food. If you have a car or bike, that's a resource. Most people have more than they realize mainly because they never stop to notice. Not you, though, because you are walking through your year with the angels! So, let's get to that list.

January 9

In order to feel part of the world you live in, it is important to find ways to contribute to it. Today is a great day to find charities or organizations in your local community that you can support. Jana says giving is a doorway to creating the world in which you wish to live. Keep in mind that this form of giving is not meant to be flashy or ego-driven at all—in fact, your donation can be small and anonymous. The point is not to receive praise for your connection but to do it so that you feel part of something bigger than yourself. So, ask yourself: What is important to you that you wish to see reflected in the community around you? Is it wanting to see a more loving community? If so, find a local organization all about love. Open this door and step through it by participating in the spreading of love. Remember that your acts of giving don't have to be sizable. Give what you can, even if it is small, and trust that whatever you can give will always be enough to make a difference.

January 10

Each new day brings with it something new, whether it is an idea or a different way to go about your day. What has worked in the past may no longer work in this new year. Think about the flow of your day. Is it working for you or against you? Today, track your activities throughout the day. See where things seem to move easily, and note places where your energy and interest wane and things seem to become harder. There is a natural rhythm to your daily experience; all you have to do is find it. There will be times of the day that are more productive than others. Find these times and use them to your advantage. Harness the energy, and let it do all the work. There will also be times in your day when it is time to rest and restore. Get into this natural flow, and your days will feel more productive, connected, and joyful.

CHECK-IN ONE

It has now been ten days since you started working with the angel Jana and the theme of doorways. Now is the ideal time to visit your altar and consider whether the items you set it up with are still relevant or you need to switch them out or add to them. It is also time to give your altar space a bit of a cleaning: freshen up any cut flowers and light your candles once more and say a small prayer or mantra, or sit in silent meditation for a couple of minutes. This small journey back to your altar will bring your mind, body, and soul back to a place of devotion and center you once again in the month's theme.

January 11

When you were a child, there were probably people whom you admired so much and wanted to be like when you grew up. The process of looking for examples of people who embody your hopes and dreams doesn't stop as you grow older. There are people you admire. There are even people you respect. Today, focus on the people who inspire and motivate you to follow your heart. These are the people who light a fire in you and make you want to make yourself and the world better. These people are your earth angels, giving you a model to replicate. While you are not meant to be *exactly* like they are—you are meant to be you—these people show you the work and commitment it takes to open your heart, be vulnerable, and step up to your divine mission, whatever that happens to be. Today, embody this level of practice and bring those inspirational figures into your awareness.

January 12

Where do you feel at peace? It is important to find places that make your soul feel at home—a space that feels as though it was designed just for you. For some, these places require traveling a great distance. For others, they are just around the corner. No matter where your space is, think today about putting time on your calendar to visit it this year. Soul homes need to be visited as often as possible, as they heal you in a powerful way. If yours is some distance away, plan your visit carefully and make sure you get as much time there as you can. If the place is just around the corner, make a conscious effort to visit it often. Mark it on your calendar and make a commitment to this experience now— don't let it slip through your fingers for yet another year.

January 13

Whether you like to admit it or not, you have karmic work to do. All humans do, and it is why you are here. Today that work is going to be a part of your path, so be aware and on the lookout for signs. These signs could include feeling as though things are harder to get through than normal or a feeling of appre- hension about doing something. You may get feelings of déjà vu creeping into your daily tasks, or it might be that you have just been in this spot before and you didn't do so well last time. Just know each time you come back to this experience and this karmic work, you are in a different place. You have worked through this before but in a different way and on a different level. Today, you may actually have a breakthrough. This particular difficulty has run its course, and now you get to move on to whatever's next. In other words, one karmic door will close, and Jana will open another for you to walk through.

January 14

Not all change happens quickly; most changes take quite a long time to process before they are even noticed. You have an opportunity here at the beginning of your year to plant the seeds for something you would like to see change by the end of the calendar's cycle. This is a change you can be patient and tolerant about, one you are more concerned with getting done correctly rather than quickly. This is a change that you will want to stick with for years to come. And this change will not just affect you, but those around you too, so now would be a good time to map out the possible consequences of that change. Start by being clear on what change you wish to seed. Ask why it is important to get it right. Then look at who else might be affected and how your change will improve their lives as well. This is yet another doorway, so make sure you know exactly what you want before you cross the threshold.

January 15

When it comes to setting the tone for your day, you only ever need to ask one question: "How do I want to feel today?" The answer to this simple question will send a ripple through the energy matrix and start aligning people and places and things to match this feeling. Do you want to feel loved? Hold your hand over your heart and claim it, by saying: "Today I will feel loved!" Perhaps you want to feel productive; place your hand over your heart and proclaim it: "Today I will feel productive." Make a decision right now on how you want to feel today. Keep it simple; claim only one feeling. Place your hand over your heart, close your eyes, take a nice, slow, deep breath, and allow the feeling to wash over you as you proclaim to Jana which door you wish to have her open. Then, move through your day and watch as the magic of your words shape your experience.

January 16

Today, take things slowly. There is no rush and no urgency. Slow and steady really does win the race. Most people are in such a rush; they want everything now! However, great things, spectacular things are born out of quiet, still, mundane moments. This energy builds over time, slowly spinning conditions into being. Then, when the moment is right, some event will burst forth into your life, and it seems so unexpected and so out of the blue. The truth is that you have been building this vortex of creation just by taking your time and enjoying your life. Relax today. Take it easy, and let the magic that is interwoven into the mundane start spinning something miraculous for you.

January 17

Not everything in your life needs to be done right this second. Your life was never meant to be one giant to-do list, filling up all the time you have in your short physical incarnation, rushing from one task to the next. What if instead you made more moments to just be—to watch the wind dance across the leaves, to observe the unfurling of a flower, or to stand in the sun and feel its rays upon your skin? Today, instead of striving for productivity, be fully present in your body and engage completely with your environment. Taste your food. Smell the seasonal smells in the air. Listen to the birds and find wonder in all that surrounds you.

January 18

Sometimes things have to wait. The solution is not always available in the moment we want it, and space needs to be created for things to align. Today is going to be one of those days. There will be things in your day that you will not be able to fix, or at least not straightaway. You have to be patient. Ask Jana to open a door so the solution can walk through it, and then trust that it will show up. On days like this, a work-around is not going to give you the result you require. What you need is resolution and not a quick fix. Walk away from problems that need more time, and allow the angel to bring any missing pieces to you to and assist in melting frustration and anger that may have been getting in the way.

January 19

Leave a door open today—a miracle may walk through it. Once upon a time, dwellings did not have so many doors. There were not as many ways to shut out, block, or close the path to the energy of miracles. There are many doors in modern dwellings; many of them are very secure and designed to keep everything and everyone out. Today, think of a miracle as a visitor: there needs to be a way for this visitor to enter your life. It not only needs permission to enter but also needs access to the area in which it will work its magic. If everything in your life is closed off, how will your miracle get in? Today, open at least one door you keep firmly shut, even if it is open for only a couple of minutes. As you open this door, say the following: "Welcome, miracle! I have been waiting for you. When you are ready, please come in and let's get to know each other." When you feel inclined, shut the door once again.

January 20

Successful people have one thing in common: a great team. Whether it's success in health, wealth, love, or their career, if someone is flourishing in life, you can bet they aren't getting those amazing results on their own. They have built a team of teachers, mentors, coaches, accountability partners, and others to help them reach their goal, whatever and whoever that happens to be. Now it's your turn. It is time to think about what sort of support you need for this year, and the goals you would like to achieve will determine this. Do you want to learn to paint, draw, rock climb, paddleboard, surf, ski, invest in the stock market? You are going to need to find good teachers. If you want to write a book, start a business, create success habits, you will need coaches and mentors. Oh, and don't forget the angels, who make a wonderful part of any team. Today, open the door to your team, even if you don't know who exactly they are yet.

CHECK-IN TWO

You have now had twenty days working with the theme of doorways and the angel Jana. It is time to pull out your journal and see how the prompts have been helping you stay in the energy of endings and beginnings. Start with this prompt: "So far this month I have _____." List some tangible results or situations where your angel's assistance has aided you. Once you are done, continue with the remainder of the month.

January 21

Devotional work is daily work, not just one-and-done type exercises. Devotional work keeps the mind, body, and energy in alignment with your highest good and your heart's desires. Devotional work can be as simple as a morning prayer, lighting a candle at some point in the day, or even pulling a tarot or oracle card to help set your daily intention. Devotional work creates a sacred pause in your day that allows you to connect with all the parts of who you are. It grounds you into your body, steadies your mind, and focuses your energy. This is why angels place feathers, coins, and other gifts on your path—to make you stop, pause, and connect. Today, remember to do your devotional work. Your body, mind, and spirit will thank you for taking a moment held in sacred pause.

January 22

Each day, you construct pieces of your life. Some of the work you do will show up in the here and now. Yet, most of it will not be fully formed until later in the future. We angels want you to be aware of what you are building today. What pieces are you putting together, and what will your finished product look like? Every repeating thought and recurring feeling is crafting your reality, building the life you will end up living. For this reason, we want you to carefully select your elements of construction. Building with sadness and fear creates a fearful and depressing future. Building with joy and laughter will build a happy and fun future. What you construct today will affect you tomorrow. Therefore, really think about what construction pieces you will gather and play with today, as this will impact the life your future self gets to live in.

January 23

Taking additional steps in a process doesn't need to translate to difficulty. Sometimes getting the exact desired results requires slowing down. Take your time. Repeat some steps, and even add some additional steps. It may take you longer to get what you want, but it doesn't make it harder to receive. Most things in life are not one-and-done; in fact it is rare and is an exception to the rule, not the rule itself. Also think about how disappointed you become when you have to repeat, slow down, take your time, and extend a process. Remember that life is on your side—it wants you to have all the things your heart desires. Some doors take more time to open, but that doesn't make them wrong or difficult doors. The right door will open in the exact right moment, offering you what you most want and more.

January 24

Check in with your body today and connect with it. Open the door to have a deep and intimate conversation with your body about how it feels. Talk to your toes, your kidneys, your liver, your arms, fingers, and every other part of you. Listen to what it is telling you, as it will have important information for you. Your body is the one thing you are connected to your entire incarnation. You can't escape it. You can't take it off and the only time you get to leave it behind is when you transition back into pure vibrational energy. By rights, your body should be your best friend. This means you need to talk to it like the long-term mate it truly is. You may even consider getting a journal to record your conversations, which could end up being one of the most helpful things you could ever do for your health and well-being.

January 25

There are days where you need to slow down and move without urgency or intensity, when you need to relax into each and every task you do. Today is one of those days. Instead of looking at what needs to be done, focus instead on what you are currently doing. Allow yourself to become one with whatever task you find yourself in the act of completing. Breathe into it. Open your senses and let the task dictate your flow. Brush your teeth one by one, really look at the dish in your hands as you dry your dishes, and put your tech toys away—instead, look into the eyes of the person you are talking to. These small, deliberate acts expand your level of awareness and connect you to the moment. They focus your mind and quiet distractions. They will also ease your anxiety and possibly even help shift you out of procrastination.

January 26

Only a fool will claim that they have learned all they need to learn. Every day brings a new lesson—like it or not, you are in the school of remembering who you are. Your physical incarnation is a school of many doors, and each one leads you back to your inner truth. With every threshold you cross, you get one step closer to your first real remembering, though you may call it "awakening." However, even remembering is not the end, not where you graduate. Reaching that point is merely the key to unlock another door with another set of remembering lessons, but that's getting too far down the road. Stick with today. What will you remember today about who you are and what you are capable of becoming? This is the quest, the mission, the reason you are here in this timeline and in this body, doing what you are doing.

January 27

When you think about how you wish to feel or be treated for the rest of your calendar year, consider putting it into practice first. If you wish to be shown kindness, you must first be kind. If you wish others to be helpful, you must be helpful to others. This embodiment of the energy you wish to receive opens the door to a very specific vortex of energy that you can spin into your new year. The vortex proclaims, "I am what I am." It makes you a magnet for what you *are* instead of what you *want*, which is really how it works anyway. Who you are will always have the strongest vibration, so be that which you wish to receive in all areas of your life. Show up as the very energy you wish to be blessed with, and watch how your world changes and shifts.

January 28

Sometimes when a door closes, you aren't expecting it. The cycle doesn't seem complete, and you feel somewhat lost and confused at this sudden ending. All the same, the door has closed and there is no going back through it. You have completed the karmic energy that was on the other side of the door. It was never about the people, places, things, or situations—it was always about what is unseen, which is also true for most of the cycles you experience while in human form. Nothing is ever sudden because you have been working through many things for lifetimes. And nothing is ever truly unexpected, as everything comes to a natural conclusion, regardless of whether your ego is ready for it or not.

January 29

There will be days where your faith wanes, where you start to doubt that the angels have your back. Things just don't seem to be going in the direction you want them to, and you are starting to feel stuck and frustrated. It is very easy when you hit one of these ruts to contract, let the negative self-talk win, and think about giving up. Angel Jana wants you to know this is the time to double down on your faith and your spiritual practices, and hold the vision of your heart's desire precious in your mind. A door is about to fly open, and if you do not stay in alignment with the energy that will push it open, you will miss it. You won't be able to spot the opening, and thus won't be able to walk into the new opportunity or possibility you have been working so hard to create.

January 30

As you move closer to the end of the month, it is time to reflect on what doors you opened and which ones you closed. Jana has been present in your life for the last thirty days. When actively working with the angel of doorways, more opportunities will undoubtedly appear. There will also be more endings than perhaps you are used to, which is why today is a day of reflection. Get your journal and write about all the new doors you have noticed this month, making sure you also write some words of thanks for them. Next, focus on the doors you have shut, again making sure to write words of appreciation for them also. This simple exercise is to raise your awareness of the many ways Jana has worked in your life over the last month. Without a moment of reflection, some of these efforts would be missed or simply go unnoticed.

January 31

It is time to say goodbye to the month and release it into the vault of memories, giving it back to the collective dreamtime. Your new year's beginning is now coming to a close. It is time to shift away from the space of the new and into the space of what is being created. You have made many choices this month that will energetically shape the rest of your year. However, this does not mean that situations and events are carved in stone, not at all. There is always space to pivot and other doors to try along the way. As the door to this month closes, just make sure the next one you open is in alignment with how you wish to feel, how you wish to engage, and how you wish to experience your next month. There are always multiple options. Choose with your heart and you will never be led astray.

Closing Ceremony for the Month

Your time with angel Jana has now come to an end for this year. It is time to pack up your altar for the angel of doorways. Give your altar a good cleaning as a way of clearing the energy you have been working with over the past month. Wash your magical items; wipe down your altar surface; and put any cards, vision boards, or images away. Remember to wave a smoking herb bundle over the space to cleanse and reset the energy, making it ready for the next angel. As you clean your altar, say a small prayer of thanks:

> *Angel Jana, I thank thee*
> *For taking this month-long journey with me*
> *For guiding me*
> *For supporting me*
> *For reminding me how to begin again*
> *I clean and clear this sacred workspace*
> *This altar I cleanse*
> *To honor you*
> *To honor the work we have done*
> *I am humble*
> *I am grateful.*
> *Thank you.*

Chapter Three
FEBRUARY

Bridgette
The Angel of Illumination

The second month of the year is when the light in the Northern Hemisphere is returning and the light in the Southern Hemisphere is waning. The dance of light between the two halves of the world illustrates what happens inside us as well. Sometimes we blaze and other times we dim. Regardless of where you live, the angel Bridgette is here to guide you in the many ways light works in your everyday life. Throughout this month, your angel is going to give you lessons, messages, and guidance related to illumination, some of which take the form of instructional tasks that will ground the lesson. The meditations, observations, and guidance itself may be more abstract because it is channeled material. Just know that whatever you personally receive from the daily prompt is correct and valid. There will be times when you need to bring more of it into your life to scare away the shadows and darkness. There will also be times where you do not need as much at all. The lessons in this chapter will show you how to summon, control, use, and even maintain light in your daily experience. Bridgette will serve you regardless of which side of the world you happen to find yourself on.

Connection Prayer: Bringing in the Energy of the Angel of Illumination

To get the most out of your month with the angel Bridgette, set up your altar for the month of February. Find a picture or pictures of a light that is burning, not one that is off or has burned out, for your altar for this month. These pictures will anchor the light energy you are calling throughout the month. I also recommend leaving space on your altar so you can add things to it as you move through your month. The daily prompts may spark (no pun intended) inspiration for things you wish to add in honor of your angel. For this month, use a yellow candle, as this color connects you to the biggest light of all, the sun. Once you have your altar cleansed and set up, light your candle and say the following prayer to bring in the energy of Bridgette and connect her to your February.

> *Angel of Illumination, I summon thee;*
> *Bring to light the parts of me*
> *The ones that long to be seen*
> *The pieces that hide within*
> *Illuminate*
> *Let your light in*
> *For this month of February*
> *Show me how to shine*
> *Burn with passion*
> *Light my desire*
> *Angel Bridgette, I invite you in*
> *Come forth this month*
> *Let us begin.*

Once you are done with your connection prayer, you can leave your candle to burn out if it is safe to do so. If not, blow the candle out and make sure you say something along the lines of: "I now blow this candle out in the knowledge that my prayer has been heard," before extinguishing the flame. Adding this statement closes your ritual and seals the sacred circle of your prayer.

Messages for the Days of the Month

February 1

Light can come in many forms. It can be as obvious as a light bulb or the sun in the sky. It can also appear subtly like a small spark, glow, or radiance from within the darkness. You are your own light. You have the ability to shine, reflect, and dim at will. You can spark yourself or be the spark for others, which means you are never really in the dark, never truly without direction or lost. As you move through this month you will learn all the magical ways you burn, sparkle, and light up the world. For now, play with your inner light and pay attention to situations where you feel yourself dim, people who light you up, and places that seem to make you radiate with pure joy. The more you notice when, where, and how your light works, the more you can refine it, play with it, and use it on purpose.

February 2

Light needs a spark or a flash—something to give it life. A flame cannot light without a burst of energy sparking first. Today, find the things in your life that spark you. What allows the light to take form in your daily habits, interactions with others, and internal narrative? You will know your spark by how it makes you feel; it will demand your attention. Your spark will propel you into action and increase ideas and positive self-talk. Expand your awareness and capture these moments. Knowing what your spark feels like will save you in your darker moments.

February 3

Finding your spark is easy; there are many things that will pique your curiosity throughout the day. The real trick is being able to keep your light lit once you have sparked it. Have you ever had to relight a candle because it did not take? Your inner light is not that different—it may need a couple of sparks from the same experience to get your flame burning. With light comes determination. Keep sparking until your inner light blazes to life.

February 4

Light needs to feed. There is a special way to nourish your light. Just as there is a special way to dim your light. To feed your light, simply look for things you appreciate. Start with the items in your room, then move on to the rest of your home, then your local community, state, country, and finally, end your mantra or chant of appreciation with things in the world you appreciate. Gravity and oxygen are good things to include in your list; without either, you can't light a fire.

February 5

There is an art to keeping a flame lit, just as there is a special way to feed a fire. In order to keep your inner light glowing, you will need to learn what it means to nourish your fire. Today, be on the lookout for things that feed your light: those conversations, thoughts, people, and places that make you glow, radiate, and shine. These are what nourish your light and keep your flame dancing.

February 6

Not everyone is able to move from complete darkness to the light. This kind of shift in energy and environment can be a shock to the system. For this reason, your angel suggests you make time in your day this month to slowly play with, nourish, and practice using your light. You could do it as part of your meditation, using your breath to feed your inner fire oxygen, or you could take yourself to places that make you feel like shining. If you have not yet marked time for the light on your calendar, now is the day to get those markers out and schedule it in.

February 7

Now that you know more about how to spark, grow, and maintain your light, let's talk about the act of being seen. One of the many reasons people like to stay in the dark is due to fear of being looked at. For some, this level of exposure can be terrifying. Yet your angel of illumination wants to reassure you that being seen for who you are always trumps stories other people make up about you, especially when you live in the shadows. Today, be open to the possibility of it being safe to be seen. You do not need to believe it just yet—for now, plant the seed and give it permission to grow.

February 8

How do you want to be seen today? What part of yourself will you allow to be exposed and vulnerable, and why? The more you work with your light, the harder it will become to stay hidden, to remain in the dark. At this point, you still may not be ready to be completely illuminated. Letting yourself dance in the light piece by piece is a wonderful way to let your seed of safety grow. Today, pick a piece of you that is itching to dance, that wants to move into the light and be seen by someone who is not you.

February 9

There is an important lesson that your angel wants to teach you this month: the difference between light and heat. Not all light gives off heat, and not all heat has a light source. And yet, they come from the same spark. Knowing when to shine and when to burn is a crucial lesson when working with your inner light. Being able to shine without burning out is necessary for your well-being. Today, practice focusing on the heat that results from being illuminated. Increase the spark's power so that it can heat your body, mind, and soul. Allow yourself to burn for a short time, like a sunburst throughout your day. Notice how it feels and how much energy is needed to maintain it.

February 10

Fire requires oxygen to burn. Breath and fire go hand in hand. Often a new spark needs to be gently given the breath of life in order for it to catch and burn. Your fire is the same. Your breath helps grow it, maintain it, and even snuff it out. So how well are you breathing and how aware of your breath are you? As you move through your day, notice how you are breathing when you feel hot, cold, and when someone comments about your glow or light. This will let you know how your breath is affecting your illuminated self.

CHECK-IN ONE

It has now been ten days since you started working with the angel Bridgette and the theme of illumination. Now is the ideal time to visit your altar and consider whether the items you placed on it are still relevant or if you need to switch them out or add to them. It is also time to give your altar space a bit of a clean: freshen up any cut flowers, light your candles once more, and say a small prayer or mantra, or sit in silent meditation for a couple of minutes. This small journey to your altar will bring your mind, body, and soul back to a place of devotion and will center you in the month's theme.

February 11

Your angel knows that the more you play with the idea of light, the more you may notice others recognize you this month—which was really her point all along, that the rest of the world could see you as radiant as she does. You may welcome this feeling, finally feeling acknowledged and possibly even validated. Or maybe you are not a fan of being seen quite so much as you are right now. You may even feel somewhat exposed. Just know that regardless of where you are on your light journey, what you are experiencing right now is temporary. How you feel today is not how you will feel next week or month. Do not stop playing with your light based on your very temporary emotional response.

February 12

There is a wonderful side effect to allowing your light to be seen: clarity. The more you move out of the dark and into the light, the clearer your life and the world around you becomes. Doubt begins to fade when things are easy to identify, which means that making decisions becomes easier. When you stand in the light and become it, there is no place to hide anything. This level of clarity will only expand as you continue your work with the light. Be careful, however—it may lead to another interesting side effect: confidence.

February 13

Welcome to a day of blessings. Follow the light today and you will surely be gifted with magic. Don't expect fireworks, however; the magic will be mundane, simple, and easy to miss. Then again, that is exactly what magic is: ordinary. Let go of your preconceived notions and, instead, let the light lead you along the path of simple blessings. You never know what small thing could have the most profound effect on the rest of your day, month, year, or even life.

February 14

What does it mean to be a seeker of the light? We sometimes confuse light with truth; although illumination can expose the truth, they are not one and the same. The light most people seek outside themselves is the light they would find if they turned inward, because what the seeker is actually after is the radiant self, the inner spark, the light that sparks when the divine self moves and takes a physical form. In many respects, it is your traveler's light. Today, stop looking outside yourself; turn your focus inward.

February 15

The light does not have to be something you stand in 24/7. In fact, there are moments where you might need to be in the dark of the world so you can see your own light shine. If you are feeling the need to be alone to tend to your own fire today, just know that is perfectly okay. When your personal inner spark is being attended to, you are adding to the larger light in the world.

February 16

If you are an early riser, you will notice an interesting contrast of light just before the sun peeks over the horizon line. It seems as though the street lights are brighter than normal and the sky feels much darker. Though perhaps not a scientific fact, it does seem as though this space is where you will find the brightest of lights. Here, just before dawn, is where those lights will be illuminated for the rest of the world to see. These are the lights that require contrasting elements to allow them to shine the brightest. In this place, your angel wants you to see how not all things need to align for you to shine. Sometimes the brightness is in the contrast, where things don't seem to match up or even make sense that your light might be at its brightest. In the contrast, the light becomes a beacon of hope, promising that more light is on its way.

February 17

Today, your angel wants you to refine your knowledge around radiant light and heat. When the angels speak of light, they are talking about radiant light, the divine light in all sentient beings. This light can shine as brightly as it wants to and no one will ever be burned or harmed. In fact, your radiant light is quite healing, both for you and all those who bask in it. Heat tends to get intertwined with light because of your connection with the sun and fire. These two things provide both light and immense heat and they do burn. So do not let the fear of burning out, or causing someone else pain, stop you from expanding your light. Unlike the sun, your radiant light is completely safe.

February 18

Contrast is a beautiful thing. It is what is required for all light to be at its most visible. Where there is opposition will be some of the brightest light. Where there is difference there will be a symphony of lights. Contrast doesn't mean conflict; more to the point, it doesn't *have to* be defined that way. Today, rejoice in the contrast you find, harmonize with different lights to yours, and see how the world can be a beautiful place when everyone allows their own light to shine.

February 19

Light can teach you how to stay focused on what is right in front of you. If your light is not very big, it will not be able to keep the shadows out of your peripheral vision. In order to keep your mind in the light, you will need to focus on what is directly in front of you. What is being illuminated in the here and now? Staying with the light and moving with it will prevent you from drifting into the past with the shadows behind you, or drifting into the unknown shadows before you, the unknown future you are creating. This is just another way to be the light, be present, and keep your focus only on what you are lighting up around you.

February 20

Shadows can teach us a lot about how we feel: they can stoke our anxiety just as easily as they can calm us down. Your reaction to the shadow areas in your life is a direct response to how well you control your light. If you have good command over your light, you won't fear the shadows because you can blast them away at a moment's notice. If, however, you find yourself contracting when the shadows approach, you need to do more active work with your light. Your light is like a muscle. The more you use it, flex it, and work it, the stronger it will become. Watch today and see if you will pass the shadow test or if you need to go back to the gym of light.

CHECK-IN TWO

You have now had twenty days working with the theme of illumination and the angel Bridgette. It is time to pull out your journal and see how the prompts have been helping you stay in the energy of the light. Start with this prompt: "So far this month I have _____" and then list some tangible results or situations where your angel's assistance has aided you. Once you are done, continue with the remainder of the month.

February 21

Heat and light go together, even though heat is not needed for there to be light. A little heat in life is not a bad thing at all. Today you may feel that heat as you are guided to act, show up, move, and be more assertive in specific areas of your life. You will know you are in the right place and taking the right course of action when you feel lit up, beaming with light. When you feel this way, it is time to act.

February 22

It is important to have a personal practice that will allow light into your life even when you don't have time, when your to-do list seems to be growing like an out-of-control monster. You need something simple that reconnects you to the light. Today, think about a two- to three-minute activity you can do first thing in the morning to connect you to the light. Is it lighting a candle and meditating with it for two minutes? Is it opening all the blinds in your home and allowing yourself to bask in the sun briefly? Write out your special light ritual and start making it a daily practice.

February 23

Your angel wants to remind you that you have the power of millions of stars radiating in your entire body, which means there are many conditions that must align in order for you to shine. Not one, not two, but millions. You are probably doing it right now and aren't even aware you are shining. Today, take note of two or three instances where you feel yourself light up, perhaps where someone told you that you seemed to shine or radiate. Or maybe you recall someone commenting on how you light up a room. Consider these experiences good evidence of the work you have been doing this month. Your angel knows that the more evidence you are provided, the more you believe in your power.

February 24

There are going to be times where your mind will not choose to look for evidence of light in your life. Instead, it will only seek darkness and things that reinforce the need to dim your light. It is up to you to retrain your mind, to raise your awareness and not allow yourself to fall back into mindlessness. Let the mind lead but do not rewrite its script, lest it become directed by ego. Remember, too, that the ego's job is not related to your soulful expansion but staying alive by any means possible. For this reason, Bridgette wants you to make a list of all the places you found light today, be it in another person, a situation, or even yourself. Redirecting your mind to seek evidence of light and not dark will train it to find more.

February 25

Today you may find yourself wanting to blaze and burn brighter than you have before, testing your light to see where its limits lie. Just remember that light can blaze in two very distinct ways: with anger and fear, and the illumination of you and everything around you in joy, love, and passion. We suggest the latter. Try testing your fuel: see exactly how much joy you can handle. Test the limits of your passion. And spread your unconditional divine love as far as you possibly can. When you understand how much of these three things you can tolerate, you will also understand the capacity of your anger and fear to limit them.

February 26

Do you know where your light ends and the shadows begin? The space where they merge is important, for it is itself neither light nor dark. It is an in-between space where both light and dark come together in a marriage of unity and wholeness, where sacred space is offered for both elements to be whole and complete. Today, find this space inside yourself, where the light and shadow parts of yourself merge. It is the space of wholeness and non-judgment that, when you can locate it in yourself, you can identify in others. What a world it would be if everyone could find that space in each other. For today, start with yourself: learn to honor you first. Then and only then, move on to honoring that space in those around you.

February 27

You have worked with the light in a number of ways this month, sometimes in a more practical way, oftentimes in a more abstract way. Yet over the course of this month, you will have found one way of working with the light that you prefer above others. Your angel wants you to focus on that today and see if you can expand or deepen your work with the light. Perhaps it could be seeing how to build light inside yourself through meditation. Maybe it was your morning altar work and connecting with the light through lighting a candle. Or maybe you have enjoyed finding places that make you feel filled with radiant light. Find your personal light connection activity today and give yourself permission to explore it further.

February 28

All month long, you have worked on building your light, maintaining it, and exploring how to shine. However, there will be days like this one, where you will need to shine your light internally, not out into the world. Today, dim your light and move it inward for some self-care, self-examination, and self-inquiry. See that whatever happens outside of you starts inside you. Make sure that what is happening inside you is exactly how you wish it to be. Shine your light on every corner of your inner world, top to bottom, side to side, front to back. Leave no area of yourself unexplored. When you know yourself, you will know how to shine.

Leap Year Day—February 29

Every so often, something special comes along, something that is only illuminated briefly. Don't be fooled into thinking that because something is special it will be easy to see. If anything, something that is unfamiliar or is not instantly recognizable can go unnoticed in your field of vision like dust in the wind. For this reason, you are being asked to stay on the lookout for anything unusual and uncommon today. It has the potential to make your light radiate in ways you never thought possible. It is something that, once gone, you will have to wait another four years to seek out again. Expand your awareness today. Be open to seeing something new, something that feels familiar but is not. Use your attention like a radar and you will be blessed with a miracle.

Closing Ceremony for the Month

Your time with angel Bridgette has now come to an end for this year. It is time to pack up your altar for the angel of illumination. Give your altar a good cleaning as a way of clearing the energy you have been working with over the past month. Wash your magical items; wipe down your altar surface; and put any cards, vision boards, or images away. Remember to wave a smoking herb bundle over the space to cleanse the energy and reset it, making it ready for the next angel. As you clean your altar, say a small prayer of thanks:

> *Angel Bridgette, I thank thee*
> *For taking this month-long journey with me*
> *For guiding me*

For supporting me
For reminding me how to shine and play with my light
I clean and clear this sacred workspace
This altar I cleanse
To honor you
To honor the work we have done
I am humble
I am grateful.
Thank you.

Chapter Four
MARCH

Willow
The Angel of Manifestation

Welcome to March, the month of manifestation. Many of you may already have your own manifestation techniques. Some of you may even be well-versed in Abraham Hicks's "Ask, Allow, Receive" principles. Willow, your angel of the month, wants you to open your heart to even more ways to play with the law of attraction. She would very much like you to play, have fun, and not take too much of this month seriously, as she believes that manifestation works best when we are enjoying ourselves. Throughout this month, your angel is going to give you lessons, messages, and guidance around manifestation that could take the form of instructional tasks to ground the lesson. Because the material is channeled, you will sometimes read meditations, observations, or guidance that may seem more abstract. Just know that whatever you receive from the daily prompt is correct and valid. Consider this month of manifestation as a month of experimentation: you will see what tools, tips, and techniques work best for you personally. One of the more frustrating elements of manifestation is comparison, so remember that whatever works for you may not work for someone else. For this reason, Willow wants you to relax and think of manifestation as a game.

Connection Prayer: Bringing in the
Energy of the Angel of Manifestation

To get the most out of your month with Willow, set up your March altar as described in the introduction. Make sure you include a collection of images that represent what you wish to manifest this month, but do your best to keep things smallish—you want to give your manifestation energy to as few things as possible. I also recommend leaving enough space on your altar to add things as you move through your month. Once you have cleansed your altar and set it up, light your candle. Say the following prayer to bring in the energy of angel Willow and connect her to your March.

> *Angel of Manifestation, I summon thee;*
> *Come play with me*
> *Let's explore*
> *Show me fun ways to invite in more.*
> *As I connect to you*
> *And you connect to the month of March*
> *I know more play is on the way.*
> *Show me, angel, how to relax*
> *How to trust*
> *That what is said will be done.*
> *Ask*
> *Allow*
> *Receive*
> *Show me the ways*
> *Angel Willow.*
> *Now with this prayer complete*
> *Let the games begin.*

Once you are done with your connection prayer, you can leave your candle to burn out if it is safe to do so. If not, blow the candle out and make sure you say something along the lines of: "I now blow this candle out in the knowledge that my prayer has been heard," before extinguishing the flame. Adding this statement closes your ritual and seals the sacred circle of your prayer.

Messages for the Days of the Month
March 1

There are so many seeds of desire around us just waiting to manifest. This month, however, your angel is asking you to choose only a few seeds to plant. Choosing might mean reviewing your list of wants and cross-referencing them with your list of needs and then seeing which ones light you up with joy. Today's task can be as whimsical or serious as you need; your angel only wants you to trust that the seeds you decide on are the correct ones for this month's journey.

March 2

Now that you have sifted and sorted your seeds, which one did you pick and how did you decide which seeds made the cut? Today, your angel wants you to journal about your seeds and why these ones out of all your manifestation options will be the ones you will plant, tend to, and allow to grow. Your journaling time will bond your energy to the soul of your seeds.

March 3

Today is the day to decide where you wish to plant your manifestation seeds. Consider the soil you will use, the amount of light the seeds will need, and what sort of watering and feeding they require. Your angel knows that these elements are metaphorical in nature: light might be radiant light, water might be your seed's emotional needs, and the soil could be your mind. Each seed will require its own unique sprouting conditions. Take your time today as you observe your world and select the best possible places to plant your seeds.

March 4

Today it is time to prep your soil for planting. Not all seeds like the same soil; some like more grit and better drainage, so their roots never have to stay wet. Others like the moisture and need it to grow. Consider that you may have to add or mix up the soil for your seeds to give them the best chance at sprouting and growing. The soil is one of the most important parts of growing the seeds in your manifestation garden, so take your time. Do not rush this process.

March 5

Having done your due diligence, it is time to finally put your seeds in the ground or, more to the point, plant them into your mind and align them with your beliefs, desires, and values. Your angel wants you to imagine physically planting these seeds and visualize the planting and sowing experience during your meditation. See them sprouting and growing healthy and strong. Imagine them bursting with life and being resilient against pests and storms. Infuse all of these energies into your seeds as you plant them to ensure they have the best start.

March 6

Now that your seeds are planted, it is time to wait. It's hard, but waiting is really a game of expanded awareness plus imagination. Every day, check your seeds: perform a quick, two-minute meditation and visualize yourself walking around your manifestation pots and monitoring your planting conditions. Make sure your thoughts, feelings, and actions (the growing conditions for your seeds) are optimal. Needless to say, there is a tremendous amount of faith involved here, and you can count on your angel to assist you in tending to these seeds.

March 7

One of the first rules of gardening is to check your seeds daily, even if you don't see any growth yet. Part of letting your seeds grow is visualizing them already grown and tending to them as if they have already sprouted. Today, check your seeds. See them grown and speak to them as though they can hear you.

March 8

Have you ever been tempted to dig up your seeds to check on them? This impatience can cause very real frustration and make you feel insecure about your ability to manifest. Don't listen to that insecurity—your seeds are doing exactly what they are meant to. Today, be kind and gentle with yourself as you settle into this waiting period.

March 9

Waiting in this holding pattern for your seeds to burst through the earth is the perfect time to think about the consequences of your dreams coming true. Most people dream big but keep the small life they have become comfortable with. Dear one, this doesn't need to be the case: the bigger your dream seed, the bigger the change to your life. For now, start preparing.

March 10

Now that you know there will be some form of price to pay for your dreams coming true have you decided what you are willing to let go of and what you will not? Start a list of all the areas your manifestation seeds affect, then make another list of the things you will not change under any circumstances and a list of the things you will. This is going to help you refine your dreams and prepare your life for the changes that are about to happen.

CHECK-IN ONE

It has now been ten days since you started working with the angel Willow and the theme of manifestation. Now is the ideal time to visit your altar and consider if the items you set it up with are still relevant or if you need to switch them out or add to them. It is also time to give your altar space a bit of a clean: freshen up any cut flowers and light your candles once more. Say a small prayer or mantra, or just sit in silent meditation for a couple of minutes. This small journey back to your altar will bring your mind, body, and soul back to a place of devotion, centering you in the month's theme once again.

March 11

Conditions in a garden change moment to moment, so make sure you are vigilant. You may be surprised to see that things have changed around your seeds. The soil might be dry or in need of aeration to make sure the correct amounts of light and oxygen are getting to your seeds. Just remember the conditions in which your dream seeds grow dictate the results you will reap.

March 12

Congratulations—you have signs of life! Your seed has sent the tiniest of green shoots out through the soil. This means you have done well in keeping your seeds well nourished. But now the hard part begins: now that your seed has sprouted, it is vulnerable and will need even more care and attention. This is a good thing; it means things are growing.

March 13

Now that your seed is bursting with life, it is more vulnerable than ever. If anything can go wrong, now would be the time. The new life is unstable, weak, and needs more care than your seed ever needed. There are many outside influences that threaten its growth: fear, complacency, and neglect, to name a few. As you move through your day, be mindful when one of these three predators enters your thinking. Protect your seeding and be fierce in your care. Remain aware of the gentle and vulnerable energy this new manifestation brings to your day. Your mantra for the day is: "I protect my dreams as they slowly begin to grow."

March 14

Did you know that all seedlings look the same at first? It is not until they get their first pair of parent leaves that they start to resemble the plant they will eventually become. Your dream seedling is finally getting its first set of parent leaves, the first of many. These leaves are the first steps to this seedling growing into the dream you planted. Slowly but surely the colors, textures, and shapes are taking form. However, the seedling is still very vulnerable to outside forces—it can still be crushed at any moment. While there is good reason to rejoice today, do not pause in your vigilance. Make sure you are reciting your mantra from yesterday and guarding your thoughts and feelings so that they stay focused on nourishment and enrichment.

March 15

Once your seedling has grown stronger, it is time to pot it, giving it its own space to grow. Your angel Willow says to select the strongest seedling to move, the one that stands the greatest chance of making it on its own. This seedling has manifested with the ability to grow fast and be resilient. If your dream is to continue its journey in the physical world, this is the seedling you want give your full attention to. You can leave the other seedlings to naturally return to the universe once you have shifted your focus away from them. Carefully remove the small plant, making sure to carry it by its adult leaves and look for the perfect conditions for it to grow into the dream it is destined to become.

March 16

Now that your dream seedling has been moved to its forever home, check its conditions and surroundings. As angel Willow reminds us, circumstances shift and move all the time. What was once going well can take a bad turn in a blink of an eye. She wants to remind you, however, that shifts don't happen without cause. In order to maintain the growth you are seeing in both your seedling and your daily life, you must stay focused. Be disciplined with your attention and nourish your mind so your awareness does not wane, as these are what can change the outcome of a destined dream. Remember that your seedling has not yet fully grown or reached its divine potential. It is up to you to make sure it does.

March 17

Your seedling is now to the point where it can get by on its own little root system. The amount of care and attention you need to pay it has dramatically decreased because it is now firmly rooted into your daily experience. It is now time to start looking for signs of new growth in your life. How is growth showing up in your daily experience? Today, your number one task is to be on the lookout for growth and note how and where it is presenting itself to you. Make sure that any growth is happening in the area of your life in which your dream seed is rooted and not somewhere else. It can be easy to forget what direction you are meant to be headed with all these new and exciting things happening in your life.

March 18

Your angel wants to remind you about the law of opposition. Your dream seed is now pretty much self-sustaining, and energy is gathering to help it bud and eventually bloom. However, there is another energy growing right alongside it: the energy of opposition. This is the energy that wants to drag you away from your goal, keep you where you are, and entice you away from growth. This law plays out in every area of life every day, but it is extremely powerful when we are working to grow, achieve, or experience something new. As you move through your day, be on the lookout for people, situations, and opportunities that may appear due to this opposing law. Make an effort to identify the correct course and keep your focus, energy, and attention on your dream seed.

March 19

Your dream seed has grown into a beautiful plant, vibrant and full of life. And it's not just you who sees this new energy bursting forth in your life—others have started to notice and are talking about it. Not all will be doing so in a good, supporting way. It is up to you to start practicing detachment from outside approval. Remember that your plant has yet to bloom; your manifestation is not complete. Think of gossip or unfriendly banter from others as pests, ones that want to eat away at what you are growing. Detachment works to repel these pests, so imagine picking all the fears, doubts, and jealous remarks off your healthy plant and flicking them away. The better you get at practicing detachment, the more your manifestation will continue to grow.

March 20

Your plant is budding—what a joy this is! A flood of positive energy is now filling your life. Everywhere you turn, good things are happening. This new trend might bring with it some tension, especially if you are not used to having so many good things happen at once in your life. Today, watch your thoughts. Be mindful of tension around you and in you. When you find yourself deflecting, or getting argumentative, stop yourself and take a breath. Let yourself pause and remember that you are just not used to feeling this good for so long. Remind yourself that this new state is not fleeting—you can feel like this for as long as you want. Keep breathing out the tension of your day and let the old past feelings go. Give them to Willow so the energy can be recycled into something more supportive.

CHECK-IN TWO

You have now had twenty days working with the theme of manifestation and the angel Willow. It is time to pull out your journal and see how the prompts have been helping you stay in the energy you are manifesting. Start with this prompt: "So far this month, I have _____" and then list some tangible results or situations where your angel's assistance has aided you. Once you are done, continue with the remainder of the month.

March 21

Today, you may feel as though the tension around your expansion is lifting. Do not let your guard down just yet. As you move through today, notice whether you or someone around you is hypercritical. This sort of snippy emotional state can trigger a cycle of tension in you all over again. It is important to understand that hypercriticism is residual energy lingering from the tightness that your manifestation has in its budding stage. But as that bud opened and the tension loosened, the feelings didn't automatically go away; they tend to recede slowly, like the tides. Spending more time than you may like on the shore of your daily experience. As you feel the hook of judgment pull at you, resist giving in. Instead, lean into the pull and breathe through it. Do not respond mentally, verbally, or even emotionally—merely identify, acknowledge, and breathe.

March 22

Your manifestation plant is starting to bloom. Some of the flowers have finally released their tension and have burst open. Things around you will look different today. You will *feel* different today, as if things just seem to go right everywhere you turn. There will be a lightness in your day that you have not experienced in a while that makes for a pleasant and enjoyable experience. Be on the lookout for soul-aligned opportunities—these are what you have been waiting for all this time. You are now ready to accept what comes your way: you are prepared, capable, and eager to start this new chapter.

March 23

Your life may seem too good to be true, but it is not. This is what a life in bloom looks like once you have walked all the steps along the path of manifestation. Your dream seed is in full bloom now. All the flowers on your manifestation plant are open and, with them, all the doors you thought were closed. The obstacles that once blocked your path also appear to be cleared. Do not waste time wondering if this is all too good to be true. You created this moment, so it's time to get busy: take advantage of every opportunity that comes your way. Say yes whenever and wherever you can. Most importantly, allow yourself to feel this moment. Soak in the feeling of victory, success, and joy—they do not have to be fleeting things. Imprint your current feelings on your memory and allow them to re-code your very being so you can repeat this day whenever you'd like.

March 24

Congratulations! You have another day of manifested miracles at your fingertips. Your flowers are still blooming, the sun is still shining brightly on your path, and all doors are illuminated. Just know that the dream seed you planted for a very specific purpose is now ready: it is now time to take the steps, open the doors, and have the conversations that bring that seed to completion. Having a life in full bloom can be distracting, so don't veer away from your intent. Instead, double down on your efforts and make sure you have the best possible experience today. As you take action toward all these manifested opportunities today, keep this mantra in your mind: "This or something more." See how the rest of your miraculous day unfolds.

March 25

Like all flowers, once your manifestation has bloomed, it will start to die after having fulfilled its divine purpose. Your manifestation seed has grown and bloomed. Now, it is starting its death sequence. The petals from your flowers are falling and the energy from your plant will fade with each passing day. Now is the time to give deep, heartfelt gratitude for all the blessings that have come your way this month. With your journal and a pen, write out everything that magically came into your life this month. Make sure you add opportunities that appeared as consequences of this magic in addition to the action steps you took to make sure you got the most out of your manifestation seed's gift. You may need to keep your journal with you throughout the day as more blessings may cross your mind. As the angel Willow knows, once you start looking for things to be grateful for, more will appear.

March 26

The flowers on your manifestation plant have all gone. The leaves are now falling, and what was once a beautiful sight to behold is looking a little on the sickly side. Today is the day to pull your plant out of the ground. The manifestation is complete, and the seed has given all it can give. This is the first phase of your manifestation cycle ending, so you may notice other things in your life today showing signs of finishing or winding down. This is a natural part of the cycle that indicates that what was once flourishing has now come to a close. Today, practice letting go. See an ending peeking its head above the horizon line to say "thank you" before it departs.

March 27

Today is a day to say goodbye. Your manifestation plant is gone; your seed has broken apart and returned to the earth. Your time with this energy vortex is over. There will be many things in your world today that will require you to say goodbye. Angel Willow wants you to remember that "goodbye" is a form of "thank you," a way of honoring what was but won't be again. It is a small ritual wrapped in two little words: "good," referring to a positive experience, and "bye" as an expression of gratitude for the energy your experience provided. Do not see these farewells as something to mourn—instead, consider them a sign of celebration. These endings are grand offerings to the Divine for a job well done.

March 28

Today we focus on things that need to be organized, tidied, and cleaned up. It is important to clear, clean, and cleanse a space once a cycle has completed. Look for pockets in your life that need a good sweeping. Remember that cleaning up doesn't have to be boring: make a playlist, invite a friend over to help, and have yourselves a tidying-up party. Don't leave energetic loose ends hanging—they will come back to smack you later. It is normal that after being busy with opportunities, other small tasks will be forgotten. Now is the time to attend to those things. Grab a cloth, a bottle of all-natural cleaner, and show the dust bunnies who's boss.

March 29

Non-action is one of the most powerful things you can do (or not do, however you wish to look at it). Today is your day of doing nothing. You do not have to act, make any decisions, or show up to places you don't wish to be. Float through your day and see what happens. Let go and sink into that lovely nothingness, the space in between what was and what will be. You find yourself exactly in a place that, incidentally, is magical. You may be surprised what miracles cross your path today while you kick back and do nothing at all.

March 30

This may feel like a bit of an odd day; there is not a lot to do, you are winding down near the end of the month, yet you are not at the finish line just yet. You may even find yourself feeling somewhat sleepy today as your energy prepares to release the month you have just journeyed through. The best way to approach today is to let it unfold and go where the energy leads you. Instead of thinking about how you want to direct your day, allow the day to show *you* the way. You never know—maybe your manifestation seed has left one last gift waiting to be found. Even if not, its energy will linger for a little while longer. Rest when you need to, and hydrate often. Follow the light and let the angels lead the way.

March 31

It is the end of the month, which means it is time to review all that came to pass from the beginning to the end of your manifestation journey. You have experienced highs, where things seemed to flow and go in a positive direction. You have also experienced some lows, where you allowed yourself to get hooked on expectations. There will also have been moments where miracles and magic lit up your world. Contemplate what you would do all over again and what you are ready to say goodbye to and never repeat. Today, allow yourself time and space to relive the highlight reel of your month with Willow, your angel of manifestation.

Closing Ceremony for the Month

Your time with angel Willow has now come to an end, for this year anyway. It is time to pack up your altar for the angel of manifestation. It is important to give your altar a good cleaning, as a way of closing the energy that you have been working with over the past month. If your manifestation seed did bloom, you might also think about burning or burying your vision board or images you used on your altar, as this particular cycle has completed. Wash your magical items; wipe down your altar surface; and put any cards, vision boards, or images away. Remember to wave a smoking herb bundle over the space to cleanse the energy and reset it, making it ready for the next angel. As you clean your altar, say a small prayer of thanks:

Angel Willow, I thank thee
For taking this month-long manifestation journey with me
For guiding me
For supporting me
For showing me how to grow, bud, and bloom
I clean and clear this sacred workspace
This altar I cleanse
To honor you
To honor the work we have done
I am humble
I am grateful.
Thank you.

Chapter Five
APRIL

The Angel of Growth

Welcome to April, the month of growth. Now that you have flexed your new manifestation skills, things around you will be moving—and dare I say, growing. Much like manifestation energy, growth does better if it is intentional, usually healthier if you are strategic and purposeful with the things, situations, and areas of your life in which you would like to see growth. As you have done in the past months, areas of focus will be limited as you move through the lessons, prompts, and guidance from your angel of the month, Faith. These things could take the form of instructional tasks to ground the lesson. Because the material is channeled, you will sometimes read meditations, observations, or guidance that may seem more abstract. Just know that whatever you receive from the daily prompt is correct and valid. You might also find that you aren't always ready to explore areas that wish to grow. The angels can often nudge us to explore things the ego has blinded us to. Yet as you work with Faith and open to her prompts, these once-hidden seeds may very well catch your attention. Like all the work with your angels, you might wish to leave space for unexpected miracles this month. As things start to shift and show signs of life, you never know what will blossom and bloom right in front of your eyes.

Connection Prayer: Bringing in the Energy of the Angel of Growth

To get the most out of your month with the angel Faith, set up your April altar. Make sure you have a picture to represent the areas of your life in which you want to experience growth. Try to focus only on one or two areas, keeping in mind that whatever area you work on with your angel will have ripple effects in other areas of your life. I also recommend leaving space on your altar to add things as you move through your month.

Once your altar is cleansed and set up, light your candle. I recommend using green candles this month, as green represents growth. If you can't find green candles, white is fine (it can represent any color needed). Before lighting it, write keywords on your candle that relate to how you would like to feel as you bring in the energy of growth. When you are ready to light your candle, say the following prayer to bring in the energy of angel Faith and connect her to your April:

Angel of Growth, I summon thee;
Come to be with me for this month
Show me how to focus my energy
To bring in change
For things to grow
To foster a good vibrational frequency
Healthy and strong
Where my intention and me
Will be as one.
Angel Faith, I open to you
Give me the courage to follow through
Let's plant some seeds
And together grow something fun
So it is said
Now it has begun.

Messages for the Days of the Month
April 1

The growth of the self is not the same as manifestation of a thing, situation, or person in your life. The growth of the self requires long vision and elevated awareness of your inner landscape. It requires commitment that no matter what happens, you are in it until the transformation is complete. It's more common to give up and give in than to stay the course and grow as beings of both flesh and light. What will you do? Make the decision now so that a clear path can be crafted for your journey. If you are truly committed to growing who you are, know this: the world around you will forever change. As you are about to find out, growth has consequences.

April 2

Growth is an inside job. Down the road, it may eventually change the nature of your outward world, but most of it happens in a place where no one else will see or even notice it. That's because growth is all about you. The quest for growth generally comes off the back of success. There is a need to know yourself better, more deeply, and in more expansive ways than before. You want to know what you are truly capable of and what your limits may be. This is where growth starts, in the act of inquiry. The questions you ask about who you are and who you are capable of becoming are the steps along the path of growth. Get those questions ready— you are going to need them.

April 3

Most humans innately know that they have limits. But most do not truly understand what that means. Because of this, very few bother to find out what their limits are. They will never know where their own personal boundaries are set, let alone find out whether those lines can be moved. If you are reading this book, however, you may be curious about your own limits, wanting to know what limitation looks like for you. This is good; this is where growth starts, slowly wiggling forward. The truth is that you haven't even come close to your limits. You are capable of so much more than you can comprehend. Today, make a commitment, right here and right now, to find your edge. Take a journey to your own outer limits and see just how much room is available for you to grow and expand.

April 4

One of the most important aspects of growth is learning about yourself, getting to know things about yourself that perhaps you didn't know before. More than likely, you may discover things you suspected were true but didn't know for sure. When we make a commitment to growth, we also make a commitment to the best and worst parts of who we are. We commit to finding those best parts and get to know and work with them in a co-created way to better our lives. It's just as important to commit to getting to know our worst parts, too, so we can erase, irradiate, and reprogram them. In order to go forward, you must understand all the parts of you that keep you stuck. What keeps you stuck hooks you to the past and sabotages your dreams. Therefore today is the beginning of getting to know you all over again.

April 5

Today, pick an area of your life in which you wish to see growth. Keeping in mind that this kind of growth is more about your internal self, select an area of life where you would like growth to appear so you can track its progress. The angel Faith says that it doesn't matter which area of life you select; it will have ripple effects in all other areas as well. Most importantly, it is better to give your growth a focus or centralized target. So where do you need to grow? In your career, love life, health, education, or even spirituality? Once you have selected where you will be focusing your energy, write it down and put it somewhere you can see it every day to serve as a reminder of your commitment. Your personal agreement with yourself forms a bond for growth's sake that should not be broken.

April 6

Now that you have a target for your growth energy, it is time to think about the steps you will take to begin your growth journey. Faith cautions you to not map the entire journey—it will guide itself. Instead, focus on where you want to begin. What small action can you take today that will set this cycle of growth in action? Perhaps it is buying a book, participating in an online class, or setting out to find a teacher or mentor. Whatever it is, today is the day to do it. Yesterday, you made your commitment. Now it is time to forge ahead and show the angels that you are someone who takes commitment seriously. Starting is a powerful energy. Some people never take the first step, but you are not "some people," and angel Faith knows this.

April 7

Congratulations! Your growth cycle has begun. The wheels are turning, and your angels are rejoicing as you embark on this new and exciting journey. Just know that the road ahead is what you make of it. With that in mind, today would be a good day to practice getting your mind in order. By this the angels mean that you need to set your perception lens to the energy you wish to carry with you through this growth cycle. The angels recommend you set your lens (that is, the way you view your day) as neutral. With a neutral lens, you will enter your new area of growth without expectation and will therefore not experience disappointment. As you move through your day, take a moment to notice how you are seeing the events unfold around you and practice moving into feeling neutral about them. Your angel knows this is going to take practice, so be patient with yourself.

April 8

For things to grow in a healthy way, they need to be in a healthy environment. Today, make sure that the environment in the area of life in which you wish to see growth is healthy. Healthy things rarely come from toxic surroundings. If your environment needs to be organized, start now. Clear out anything that could contaminate or strangle your growth. Make sure your environment is kind, compassionate, welcoming, and safe. To practice, take a good look around your house first. What can you clear away, declutter, and clean up? Next, examine where you work. After that, sit in meditation for two minutes and do your best to clean, clear, and declutter any thoughts or beliefs you have around what you are wanting to grow.

April 9

Your inner voice and the way you feel are the soil in which you will plant your growth intention. If you wish to see positive results, you will need to tend to the soil. It is easy to allow weeds of past failures or old wounds to spring up and hinder your growth. These feelings can be hooked deeply in the core of who you are, existing there for so long that they broadcast their own talk radio show inside your head. If you want to have any chance of success this time around, you will need to remove those hooks and do some serious weeding. Just know that this is not a one-and-done process. The more you grow, the more aggressive the weeds can become. In fact, this is the beginning of a lifelong project—but one that your angel knows is well worth the reward it will give you.

CHECK-IN ONE

It has now been ten days since you started working with the angel Faith and the theme of growth. Now is the ideal time to visit your altar and consider whether the items you set it up with are still relevant or if you need to switch them out or add to them. It is also time to give your altar space a bit of a clean, freshen up any cut flowers, and light your candles once more. Say a small prayer or mantra or sit in silent meditation for a couple of minutes. This small journey to your altar will bring your mind, body, and soul back to a place of devotion and center you once again in the theme of the month.

April 10

Today, check for signs of growth. More than likely, you'll see something so small that if you were not deliberately looking, you would never find it. Throughout this month, you will be prompted several times to find evidence of growth energy, all while making adjustments and refinements to the way you think, feel, act, and engage. It is easy to not notice a reduction in negative self-talk, just as it's easy to overlook when calm and peace are becoming more dominant feelings throughout the day. For this reason, you will be intentional in all you do today as you scout for signs that you are indeed on the path of growth. Keep a notebook or paper and a pen handy because documenting your findings is the best way to prove to yourself that the work has begun.

April 11

When we deliberately set down the path of growth, we do so for a very specific reason. Generally, we seek growth because something in our lives is not bringing us the results we would like, mentally or emotionally. Today, clarify and reaffirm the results you are seeking. You need to be able to write them out in such detail that there would be no way to miss them if they came knocking at your door. Ask yourself why these particular results are so important to you. Why is it essential you create them and experience them? What will achieving these results give you, or what door do you believe they will open? Your angel says it's time to pull out your journal and answer these questions in an honest and heartfelt way. Your answers should reaffirm what you are asking for and refine which actions you will take next.

April 12

Today, check your boundaries. Real growth happens when you have a firm set of boundaries around your thoughts, feelings, and reactions. You need to be able to set yourself up for success as much as possible, and that entails knowing what you will and will not allow in your world while you are on this journey of growth. Ask yourself: what thoughts do you wish to no longer have? What feelings are you banishing from your experience? And what people or environments need to be limited for you to stay on the path of growth you have selected for the month? The good news is that this very act of setting clear, concise, and healthy boundaries is a sign of real, true, and lasting growth. Setting boundaries signals the end to old habits and a beginning for intentional living.

April 13

You angel knows that growth can be scary because it asks you to take risks and do things you have never done before. And you are asked to do so without any guarantees or reassurances. Growth also has far-reaching consequences, some of which are obvious, most of which are not. Growth is not for the faint-hearted— it is for the brave, the courageous, for *you*, little one. This is true even if you do not see yourself as a particularly strong person. You will take a leap of faith today, one that will stretch you as much as it can frighten you. Deep within all that worry and anxiety will be excitement, a deep well of joy laying the foundation of incredible things to come—which is why it will be easy to jump, even though there is no safety net waiting for you. We know you will learn quickly that this new phase of your life was where you needed to be all along.

April 14

It is easy to arrive at the middle of a growth cycle and feel like quitting. Do not. It is easy to look around and claim there is no evidence that things in your life are changing. But you need to remember that the world outside is the very last place evidence of your growth will show up. Instead, look inward. Notice if there is a change in how you think, feel, respond, and act in situations or around specific people. Your inner world will show you what you seek long before it will manifest in the outer world. Today, pay very close attention to your inner voice and how your mind and heart respond to situations throughout the day. Shift your focus inward and see that you have started to change, shift, and grow.

April 15

Today, your angel asks that you focus on being present, especially with people and in situations where you normally resist being fully engaged. A true sign of growth is a change in how you spend time with yourself, your work, your interests, and the people you consider important in your life. When you are present, you are grounded deeply in the moment. The more present in the moment you are, the more you can foster impressive growth and manifest a happier, more abundant future. No matter what area of your life you are working on this month, giving yourself permission to be present will only increase the amount and depth of growth you will experience.

April 16

There is no doubt that growth can be hard, even when it is something you have begun willingly. At the beginning you are motivated and ready to see changes in your life. You have acknowledged there are opportunities you would like to receive and have charted a path to grow, learn, and expand. But as the journey deepens, emotions, memories, and doubts roll in. You become less excited and motivated, and nothing seems quite as easy as it felt in the beginning. This change in feeling happens because you are starting to peel back the layers and reveal what has been stopping you from growing in this area of your life. Be brave, little one; face your fear about your current revelation. Inhale deeply and exhale, blowing your discomfort away with your breath, releasing it enough so you can move on.

April 17

Growth requires a new level of organization. What used to work before may not work now or even again as you get further on your growth journey. Today, look at the area of your life in which you have called growth forth to see where more organization is needed. What systems do you need to have in place to make the next phase of your growth cycle run smoothly and effortlessly? See if you may need to hire or ask someone to assist you in this organization. Perhaps you need a housekeeper once or twice a week regular appointments with a massage therapist, or maybe an assistant to help your business or professional life grow at its best. Go over every aspect and moving part of this area of your life and be honest about where and how this new level of organization will help elevate you and add to the growth you are looking to see.

April 18

Growth often means creating a new version of who you are. That new version might seem small when you first start this journey. However, it's common for it to end up becoming a larger experience the more you start to grow into the person you have set out to become. Start thinking about how this new you will dress and be seen. Today is a day to get playful. Thinking about how a new you will look, what shoes will this new version of yourself wear? What style and color clothing are going to be a vibrational match for the new you? Go through your wardrobe and see if you already have some pieces that give off your new growth vibes. When you find these pieces, it is important to wear them as costumes. The more you can feel the end result of your growth, the more motivation you will have to see this journey all the way through to the end.

April 19

Rest and recovery are an important element of growth. When you are in a growing cycle, you are using a lot more energy than normal. It becomes that much more important to listen to your body when it gives you signs, nudges, and indicators that it needs to take it slow. This might mean getting a few extra hours of sleep at night, clearing your schedule as much as possible so you can spend less time thinking about work or your social life. Plan and make space for those much-needed self-care days. Today is one of those days, so take it easy today.

Do not push yourself; listen to what your body is telling you. Eat lightly, stay hydrated, and allow yourself some integration time. Remember the physical body is the last place change manifests. So be gentle and kind to your body and mind.

April 20

As you look around your life today, can you identify thoughts, feelings, or actions that are out of alignment with the growth you have been working so hard on this month? Today, your angel would like you to do an audit of any parts of yourself that seem to conflict with the energy you are growing in your life. These parts either tell you that your growth journey is a waste of time or sound like little nagging voices in your head that want to derail you. You are at an important stage of your growth cycle—it will only take one small thought, feeling, or action to undo all your good work. You angel knows you are so close to achieving your goal. Today, grab that journal and take note of the thoughts or feelings bubbling up that could steer you offtrack.

CHECK-IN TWO

You have now had twenty days of working with your theme of growth and your angel, Faith. It is time to pull out your journal and see how the prompts have been helping you stay in the energy of growth. Start with this prompt and then make lists of tangible results or situations where your angel's assistance has aided you: "So far this month, I have _____." Once you are done, move on to the remainder of the month.

April 21

Today, your angel would like you to stop and pay attention to how the energy of growth is affecting your body. In a mirror, really look at your skin, nails, hair, and eyes—can you see a difference in them? How does it feel to be the custodian of your current body? When you bring your focus back to your body, you will ground the energy of your growth. Growth is no longer just a cerebral exercise—it has become something you fully embody in mind, body, and spirit. You reinforce it by simply noticing and honoring the changes this current growth cycle is making to the temple of your soul, your flesh-and-bone body.

April 22

It is time to be grateful for stability. Just as there are things changing in your life, shifting, moving, and recreating themselves to attune to your new frequency, other things are staying the same. They are solid, grounded points of reference in your life that are consistent and resilient. Today, honor these stable parts of your life and give thanks for them. You could do something as simple as give thanks to your favorite chair, your bed, your pillow. These simple everyday items help you in more ways than you can possibly comprehend. As you move through your day and these things cross your path, say thank you—that's it; two words.

April 23

Today your angel wants you to start celebrating your growth by acknowledging all the wins you have had this month, big, small, and in between. Growth isn't only measured by crossing a finish line—it is measured in the victories you have along the way. It is about acknowledging the shifts and changes you are creating in your life with every thought, feeling, and action. Have you created new habits along your growth journey? Celebrate them. Maybe you have stopped reacting to a co-worker who usually pushes you over the edge. Celebrate it. Maybe you put on real pants with a zipper for the first time in weeks. Oh my goodness, yay you! All of these and more are signs of growth. As you move through your day, be on the lookout for more things to celebrate and feel victorious!

April 24

Now that you are starting to see hints and clues in your outside world that your new growth is in full swing, it is time to ask yourself if you are enjoying the direction in which this new energy is guiding you. Is this what you wanted to happen when you set out on this journey? Is it better than you expected, or is it causing difficulties and disruption? If you'd like a hint: none of this is good, and none of it is bad—it is all consequences of your decision. And you can refine, adjust, and navigate your decisions in any way you choose. Today, remember that you are not a victim of your decisions—you are the master of refinement.

No matter what is happening in your life right now, you have the power to change, shift course, and direct your growth energy in any direction you desire.

April 25

Your angel knows you have been very strategic this month, and each day you have moved your energy, thoughts, and feelings through a high-resonance growth cycle. That takes a deep level of commitment and internal need for change. Say thank you to your mind, body, and heart for moving with you. Say thank you to your energy for supporting you and charting the course of your journey. Give thanks for the conditions and environment that assisted you in creating this new growth. Acknowledge all the people who have helped you this month and continue to stand by you as you grow. As you move through your day, be on the lookout for more things to give thanks for and wins you can add to your victory audit.

April 26

You may have noticed things moving at a much more rapid pace now than at the beginning of the month—this is normal and just means your growth vortex has picked up speed. As it gets faster, more cracks and gaps will appear in your organizational structure. This is not a bad thing; if anything, it is a positive sign that your life is not the same as it once was. However, gaps and/or cracks do require your focus and attention. Today, be observant. Create a list of all the places these gaps are showing up. Notice the need to be clearer or more concise with those around you. Then, pave the way for the solutions. You may not have all the answers today, but opening yourself up to receive them may very well result in them knocking on your door tomorrow.

April 27

When getting close to the end of a cycle, it is important to check and see that all boundaries are in place or in need of resetting, restoration, or reimagination. This is your task today. Whatever worked before this month may not be working anymore. You angel wants you to make sure you are protecting your sacred space. When things are changing in your life, it's easy to allow boundaries to loosen or slacken. Remember that your energy is important. Your feelings are vital and your mental health is paramount. Today, take some time to make sure your boundaries are solid, firm, and—most importantly—functional. If you need to reset them, do so kindly and compassionately.

April 28

Excuses can be like anchors. They keep us stuck in spaces we claim we do not wish to be. As you wind down this month, make sure that you are anchored only to a spot that nourishes and sustains your new growth. And now that you have reset your boundaries and reimagined the circle of protection around your sacred space, the task should be simple. Today, look for those stubborn points of resistance. Once you have found them, imagine yourself hoisting your anchors up to where you are now and let Faith dissolve them. More than just finding somewhere new to place any anchors, it is more important to get rid of them once and for all. Take a sip of water or another beverage after you dissolve each anchor as a way to honor its parting from your growth timeline.

April 29

Today, take some time to do a little cleaning: physical, house, or in your office space. This physical act has emotional, mental, and energetic benefits that connect and ground all the work you have done for the month. Before you start, light a candle (of any color) in honor of Faith, your angel of growth. You might even offer her a small prayer. Then, begin tidying up: remove anything you don't need and throw out any junk or rubbish you may have accumulated in the last month. Wipe down surfaces and water any plants. Sort books in your bookcases and vacuum or sweep your floors. This simple cleaning ritual will reset and restore your energy for growth, stabilizing all the work you have done this month so you may keep it moving forward. Once you are done cleaning, let your candle burn all the way down if it is safe to do so. If not, blow it out.

April 30

For a fun way to end this month, buy either a living plant or a bunch of beautiful flowers and place them somewhere special in your home or office. Bringing a symbol of growth into your space will activate the living growth energy inside you. Remember that what is inside is what is outside and vice versa. So let the outside world gloriously depict all that is moving, shifting, and growing inside of you. Your life force has an energy that is radiant, strong, and bursting at the seams with creative potential. Allow yourself to bask in this energy from your plant or flowers just as others are basking in you. Like the plant, you are brimming with light, energy, and possibility. You are a beacon of hope to all who cross your path and a living message from Faith herself to everyone who would want her in their lives for their own growth.

Closing Ceremony for the Month

Your time with Faith has now come to an end, at least for this year. It is time to pack up your altar for the angel of growth. Give your altar a good cleaning as a way of releasing the energy you have been working with over the past month. Cleanse your magical items; wipe down your altar surface; and put away any cards, vision boards, or images. If you would like, wave a smoking herb bundle over the space to cleanse the energy and reset it, making it ready for the next angel. If you bought living plants during or near the end of your month, keep them on your clean altar as a way of keeping the living energy of growth for the rest of the calendar year. As you clean and reset your altar, say a small prayer of thanks.

> *Angel Faith, I thank thee*
> *For taking this month-long growth journey with me*
> *For guiding me*
> *For supporting me*
> *For showing me how to stretch, bend, shift, and grow*
> *I offer you this living plant*
> *To keep the growth energy going*
> *I clean and clear this sacred workspace*
> *This altar I cleanse*
> *To honor you*
> *To honor the work we have done.*
> *Thank you.*

Chapter Six
MAY

Daniel
The Angel of Movement

Welcome to May, the month of movement. It is normal to switch your focus to the movement in your life after you have manifested and grown. Things in your life will more than likely be shifting all over the place, which can bring a feeling of instability. And a feeling of instability can lead to feeling unsettled and uncertain. Be careful: you don't want all that new, wonderful energy in your life to get screwed up. Luckily, you'll have angel Daniel with you for the entire month. Throughout this month, your angel is going to give you lessons, messages, and guidance-related movement that could take the form of instructional tasks that will ground the lesson. The meditations, observations, and guidance itself may be more abstract because it is channeled material. Just know that whatever you personally receive from daily prompts is correct and valid. Your angels know that the best way to leverage this energy is with an intentional plan. Over the next thirty-one days you will be guided, supported, and nudged to take the next steps and actions so that you do not lose momentum and are able to sustain and maintain all that new energy you have worked so hard to cultivate.

Connection Prayer: Bringing in the Energy of the Angel of Movement

To get the most out of your month with the angel Daniel, set up your May altar. Make sure you have a picture to represent the area or areas of your life in which you want to see movement. As you did before, try to focus on only one or two areas and remember that whatever area you work on with your angel will have ripple effects in all other areas of your life. I also recommend leaving space on your altar so that you can add things as you move through the month.

Once your altar is cleansed and set up, light your candle. I recommend using orange candles this month, as orange represents movement. If you can't find orange candles, white is fine (it can represent any color needed). Before lighting it, write a direction or result on your candle that indicates where you want to see movement and why. Your direction might be career, health, or even romance, and the end results could be signing a new contract, feeling healthier, or going on a first date. Keep your statement short; it needs to fit on your candle, after all. When you are ready to light your candle, say the following prayer to bring in the energy of angel Daniel and connect him to your May:

Angel Daniel, I summon thee;
I call you forth to guide me
Point me in the right direction
Stick my feet to the path
Show me how to move
Nudge me when I am reluctant
Hold me when I am fearful
Cheer me when I move through doubt
Light me up when things get dark.
In your presence I will trust
That all movement is for my greater good
I call you forth
Connect you to me
To this month of May.
Let us move as one
With grace and ease
With these words spoken
This prayer is now done.

Messages for the Days of the Month

May 1

Movement is a tricky energy to pin down. Sometimes what we think is movement is really a ripple effect of someone else's influence. Because movement has consequences, it can be difficult to know if any shifts you feel are yours or the result of someone close to you when first starting a journey. For this reason, you will learn what movement is and is not this month, as well as how to control it. You will learn how to ride movement's effects even when you aren't doing anything at all but are in the right place at the right time with the right set of conditions. Creating movement in your life doesn't always mean doing something, nor is it always about physical effort. You may start to see that the quickest way to get from point A to point B is adjusting how you think and feel. We have lots to cover this month, so strap your seat belts on and let's get moving.

May 2

Movement isn't always intentional; it will happen regardless of whether you set a course or not. Every single day, the actions of others mingle with the energy of your life and create movement. Sometimes we are okay with this, other times not so much. Today, identify an area of your life where you are not happy with the direction things seem to be taking. Ask yourself why you are unhappy about this movement and see if you can identify who or what you have allowed to direct the flow of this area. Consider if you have the strength and capacity to take back control and steer it in the direction you desire. There are no right or wrong choices here, only ones that bring you joy or suffering. We ask that wherever possible, choose joy.

May 3

Each day brings with it a new path to walk, a new ocean to sail, and a new adventure to have. No two days must be the same. In fact, your angel wants you to know that the more similar your days are, the less control you may have over the energy created in your life. Your angel of movement would like you to be more mindful of habitual behavior patterns that have allowed you to get stuck in repetition. If you do not explore new directions or change course once in a while, you will no longer be consciously directing the movement of your day, month, year, and life. It is easy to get stuck in this movement cycle, especially when your daily tasks seem to be the same. But just because you need to do the same thing doesn't mean you must do it the same way every single time. Today, bring your awareness back to your body and be more conscious of how you move and why.

May 4

Learning how to master movement in your life starts with plotting small paths in your days. Before you even put your feet on the floor, your angel would like you to set a course for your day. Show the energy where you wish to travel and how you wish to feel while traveling along this specific path. See yourself making your way along the course you have set out for your day. Smile as you watch yourself move from one task to the next with ease. Sigh and drop your shoulders as you visualize how easy it is to engage with whomever crosses your path today. And don't forget to breathe steady and strong. Follow this movement all the way to seeing yourself get into bed. Now that the movement of your day has been mapped, place your feet on the floor and let the energy retrace the steps of your mind. At the end of the day, record how being intentional with your movement for the day benefited you. Plan to do it again tomorrow.

May 5

In many respects, this month is about learning to drive the vehicle called your life. And Daniel, your angelic co-pilot, is making sure that all movement in your life is taking you in the exact direction you want. Of course, the more you move, the more opportunities and possibilities you will create, which means more new ways to move and drive your life will appear. For this reason, it is important to double-check the location of this month's end destination. Every new road, sign, or path you come across will tempt you. It is important to discern whether what you see will bring you closer to your destination or take you further away. Or worse—what if it keeps you moving in circles, never making any progress whatsoever? Today, reaffirm your destination and speak it aloud to Daniel. Let him be your compass, and trust that he will let you know when and where to turn.

May 6

Your angel would like you to understand that every action you take is movement—even when you take no action at all, you create a series of chain reactions because everything in your world is connected. Something as simple as saying thank you will create movement in a positive direction. Today, Daniel would like you to consider the direction of your movement. Are you moving things in your life in a positive direction by staying in the vibrational energy of joy, gratitude, and abundance? Or are you moving the energy and creating movement in the opposite direction through fear, doubt, sadness, and anger? Spend two minutes today to see where and how you are creating movement in your day.

May 7

Movement doesn't understand the ego's concept of perfection; it only knows it must direct energy in one direction or another. Yet, too often, movement in your life is blocked by your need to get it "right" or your desire to have it done "perfectly." Blocked energy still looks for a direction to move in. Eventually, that energy will create its own path, and very rarely will it be in the direction you wish for it to go. Today we ask that you consider directing your energy in imperfect ways and trust that your angel knows exactly where you want to move and why movement in this area is so important to you. Trust is the only reason for stalling, procrastinating, and blockages in your flow. Let us reassure you that no matter what you do today, it will be enough and exactly the way it is meant to be. Trust in us and all will flow.

May 8

Today your angel wants to talk to you about momentum, or having enough energy behind an idea, solution, or goal that opportunities seem to fly in all at the same time. When you first start the movement process you don't really see much happening in the world outside of you. But the more you move, you pick up speed. This speed creates a vortex of energy that starts to propel you through the world of time and matter and places you squarely at the foot of opportunity. So, little one, where and how is momentum working in your day? Take a moment to meditate on all the opportunities that seem to be unfolding for you and which ones you may need more momentum to create.

May 9

Movement clears out stuck, blocked, and resistant energy from your physical body. When energy is flowing through you, you will feel a sense of joy and freedom that will end up attracting you to the very thing you have been stressing about. Today, move it! Shake, dance, wave your arms in the air, and don't stop until you feel like you have finally moved yourself from struggle to freedom. You will notice the energy pop or shift—it is a physical sensation. You might even be surprised how quickly you let it go once you allow yourself to move, jiggle, and rock and roll. It might sound silly, but do it anyway. Find some music, turn the volume up (use headphones to respect anyone around you) and get that body moving as fast and free as possible.

May 10

Today your angel would like you to consider how movement creates connection. If you do a lot of traveling, you know how many new people you meet with each trip you take. While most of these connections are temporary and fleeting, every so often a deeper connection is made—before you know it, you have a friend for life. Today, Daniel would like you to explore how movement is creating connection in your life. Whom have you met, spoken to, enjoyed a meal with, or even befriended as a direct result of movement? These people do not need to be from travels—they could be from your decision to take a new job, go to a different cafe, or ride the bus instead of driving your car. Daniel says to follow the threads of how you have moved through your life and see what they have brought along for the ride.

CHECK-IN ONE

It has now been ten days since you started working with the angel Daniel and the theme of movement. Now is the ideal time to visit your altar and consider whether the items you set it up with are still relevant or if you need to switch them out or add to them. It is also time to give your altar space a bit of a clean, freshen up any cut flowers, and light your candles once more. Say a small prayer or mantra or sit in silent meditation for a couple of minutes. This small journey to your altar will bring your mind, body, and soul back to a place of devotion and center you in the theme of the month.

May 11

Intentional movement requires us to narrow our vision, to put blinders on to block out any and all distractions that might cause us to move our focus or change directions. Have you ever noticed how many things draw your gaze, focus, and intention away from your daily tasks? Today, make a note every time you feel yourself distracted, being pulled off task, or when someone talks you into doing something that's not at all on the path of your intentional movement. Narrowing is not as easy as you think, and the more you focus on it, the more things will come up to lure you away from your destination. Stay strong, let clarity guide you, and do your best to make it to the end of the day without being waylaid too much.

May 12

Daniel knows that sometimes it is easier to make a move in the physical world once you have done it first on the mental plane. Today, practice taking action in your head before trying it in your life in a quick visualization exercise you can do throughout the day. Imagine yourself doing the thing you want to do, going where you want to go. Next, ask Daniel to come assist you with any movement that feels difficult or scary. Breathe deep and slow while seeing yourself complete the move you wish to make. Take one last deep breath. Do this exercise throughout your day and see how different your physical and emotional bodies respond when putting mental images into action.

May 13

There will be times when you need a helping hand or two (or ten). What needs to be done to get things moving and flowing again might be bigger than you can deal with on your own. Problems of this size usually show up in places you have been ignoring, sections of your experience you have repeatedly delayed dealing with or dismissed. These feelings of aversion arise when a task requires more than just you to complete it. For this reason, Daniel is asking you to seek help today. At the very least, explore where the help you need can come from, and mark a date and time on your calendar for taking action on obtaining that help. Now is the time to face these areas of your life. Resolve the blocks and get things moving once more.

May 14

Not all moves are going to make logical sense. For the most part, movement is not linear; it tends to zig-zag, taking us on roundabout journeys that we ourselves would never logically choose. Yet our soul and karma know that erratic movement is exactly how we need to move in order to learn lessons, meet specific people, and gain a better understanding of who we are and why we are here. Daniel says we need to have a target, something to aim for. He says to be intentional with our energy and actions but remain open to how it will lay itself out. Daniel wants you to start opening up space in your journey for adventure, allowing yourself to feel the awe of how everything will eventually fall into place. In a way, the angels want you to trust that every unexpected twist and turn is a miracle upon which you will lay the foundation for your next point of personal evolution.

May 15

Consider a day where you have nothing to do—there's nowhere to go and no one wants anything from you. You are absolutely free to do what you want, when you want, and how you want. What would you do? Would you use this opportunity to sleep, sit on the couch, go out with friends, or spend time with loved ones? Or would you use it to move closer to your goal? There is a difference between people who get what they want and those who claim to want something, and that is what they do when no one is looking. Successful people have specific movement habits, which is why they seem to be achieving the impossible while everyone else is stuck on what to have for breakfast. Today you get to choose which type of person you wish to be.

May 16

Being a master of movement requires flexibility, or the ability to swiftly change direction. You are aware enough to know when you need to slow down and speed up. At the level of mastery, the manner in which you move toward your goals has an intuitive quality. This intuition allows you to be more present, focused, and grounded in the energy, thus setting the course of your day. Today Daniel asks you to tap into that energy. See how it is flowing and shifting around every action you take. He wants you to see if you can flex and flow with it rather than push against and resist the direction it wants to move you. Allow your energy to be movable today, and let the angels guide you to a path with fewer obstacles and more peace and calm.

May 17

There will be times where something unplanned comes up, a surprise that more than likely interrupts your flow in the day. The angels are asking you not to see these sorts of events as good or bad but as opportunities to move differently, to respond in ways you may not have in the past, and be more conscious of the rippling waves of consequences. As you move through your day, set the intention to not respond immediately when interruptions cross your path. Give yourself permission to pause, work through your emotional response, and consider how to move with an unexpected event in your way. Who knows—perhaps this could be the best thing to happen to you today. You won't be able to tell until you have dealt with it and gotten back on course.

May 18

There are times in everyone's life where it feels like we are going backward in order to move forward. While this isn't exactly accurate, the angels understand that it feels that way. What you are feeling is the uncoiling of the spiral you call time. You have revisited a place on your spiral that feels very familiar but is not exactly the same—*you* are not the same. The conditions, possibilities, and opportunities are thus different. New and exciting outcomes await you if you can ride the spiral wave outward and not allow yourself to cling to the past. Today might feel like one of those days. You might have been making some good progress in life, but now forward momentum seems to have stopped; at worst, you could feel yourself slipping backward. Daniel wants you to know that this is not the case. Eyes forward, take a breath, and just let the day unfold.

May 19

When things feel like they're not moving at all or time feels like it is standing still, it is easy to become despondent about your life. Angel Daniel wants you to know that in these moments, the angels are working their hardest. The action is all happening behind the scenes. While you of course cannot see it, you will be able to feel it if you pause to take a breath and drop fully into the moment. The feeling is like a slight crack in the air, like waves of energy all seeking the same target. This is the movement the angels are creating. Use this time to prepare for what is coming. Once all the behind-the-scenes work is done, it will feel like time has sped up in your life and you might find yourself moving at a pace you are not used to. Clean those running shoes and limber up—life is about to get very busy indeed.

May 20

Some movement is slower than others. For the most part, we can get very stuck on seeing things at their fastest speed; we want it all right now. The problem with this level of grasping for speed is that it doesn't allow us to breathe into the larger life-changing movements happening around us. Think about how much life changes in a ten-year period. Most of the movements that created that change happened slowly. You will be able to track peaks and valleys in momentum, but overall, things happened slowly over an extended period of time. More than likely, we simply don't notice things that don't happen at a pace that is visible in our day-to-day. But when we look back, we can accept what has happened. Daniel wants you to bring that feeling of acceptance to your day. Allow yourself to accept that the biggest movement in your life is taking place at a level that you cannot see without the assistance of hindsight. Once you do accept this fact, the stress, worry, and doubt around your daily to-do lists will diminish.

CHECK-IN TWO

You have now had twenty days working with your theme of movement and your angel Daniel. It is time to pull out your journal and see how all the prompts have been helping you stay in movement. Start with the following prompt and make lists of tangible results or situations in which your angel's assistance has guided you: "So far this month, I am creating movement in _____." Once you are done, move on to the remainder of the month.

May 21

Today you might be asked to move differently than you are used to. The angels are asking you to trust the direction regardless of where you seem to be facing. As you have learned this month, not all movement happens in a straight line, and some of it will not make logical sense without the lens of hindsight. Instead, your angel wants you start listing whenever the movement feels off, strange, disorienting, or even difficult. Something deeper might be going on that requires you to pull out your journal and explore. As you do so, be mindful to not judge your direction in the moment. Just go with that direction and document how it feels as you go. It will all make sense later when time has passed and your goal is achieved.

May 22

Just like you need to intentionally slow down, there will be times when you need to intentionally speed up. Today is one of those days. Steady yourself, hydrate, and make sure you can sustain the pace you are setting. Remember that what you are going through is a marathon, not a sprint. That said, this heightened level of energy will not be needed for very long, just to get you over the edge of the unknown. You have been so close to this edge for a while now; it's finally time to plant your feet flat on the ground and speed your way over it. You will know when it is time to relax because you will hit a point of exhilaration when you cross the threshold. Hold that feeling for as long as possible and then let it all go.

May 23

Riding the current of your previous movement is what is required today. After a day of taking such intense action, you need a coasting day. Your angel is asking you to trust that the momentum you created yesterday will be more than enough to move you through whatever today brings. Little effort will be required on your behalf. This is true for all days that follow an intense burst of energy. Because humans live in the realm of residual energy, it takes a while for the energy to catch up on the physical plane of existence—and this is one of those days where that is indeed a blessing. Allowing yourself to surf the energy current of your own action is part of learning how to flow with the movement of your life. There's no pushing, no trying to figure things out—only riding the vibe of what has already been created.

May 24

Today's angelic reminder is about how the way you feel in any given moment will create thoughts and actions that in turn spin the wheels of your momentum. Have you ever noticed that when you feel out of sorts, storm clouds seem to follow you everywhere you go, that ornery and disagreeable people seem to appear in your path left, right, and center? The same happens when you are feeling unstoppable. People, places, and things just seem to line up like magic, and everything seems to fall into place without any effort whatsoever. How you feel guides your momentum. Today you are being asked to see which emotions or feelings are directing the flow of momentum in your life. The direction you go in and which doors open or slam shut will be influenced by the emotions creating the energy of your day. Think of today as a game: play it out without judging yourself or others and see what happens.

May 25

Actively creating momentum can be exhausting. You will notice that you burn a lot of energy and your mind starts to become overwhelmed. Stress and doubt can creep in. The more tired your body, mind, and emotions become, the more you start to question why you are moving at all. Angel Daniel would instead like you to schedule days to rest so that you do not reach these moments. Days of rest mean more than just an hour or two of downtime—you need to rest, unplug, and care for your body and mind. The great thing about momentum is that it can sustain itself for a while. Taking a low-energy day or two every week will not slow or stop your forward movement. If anything, it might actually speed the process up, as you won't be so hands-on. For today, plan out your rest days. Mark them on your calendar now so you can't make excuses and skip them. Your future self will thank you for taking the time to rest, restore, and recalibrate.

May 26

Today, your angel would like you to go back to the original intention you created at the beginning of this month and see how close you are now to your destination. Follow your journey this month and see if you can map the route you took to get where you are today. Do not use this exercise as a way to pass judgment on yourself. Instead, use it to celebrate the distance you have traveled regardless of whether it is long or short. The fact that you have moved at all is something to celebrate. Give yourself a pat on the back and start casting your thoughts toward the last leg of your journey, the last few days of this month, and what you need to do in order to fulfill the intention created at the beginning of it.

May 27

There will be times when you feel like you are making incredible headway. Things seem to be moving along. Pieces seem to be falling into place, and you appear to be more productive than ever before. Then, suddenly, it just stops. It is subtle at first, as things slow down and plateau before coming to a grinding halt. One day you look around and notice all the movement has stopped. Guess what? You have arrived. While you were busy focusing on all the energy, all the shifts and turns, you forgot to be on the lookout for your original intention, which has now come to its completion. Maybe you don't feel as though you have arrived, nor may it look like you are at your destination—that is only because you lost sight of the original plan along the way. Instead, your vision changed and evolved as you created momentum. Remember that movement is a journey: you plug in your coordinates and expect to arrive at your destination. Now, it is time to punch in coordinates for your next journey. Set your course for the next leg and allow the momentum to accumulate again.

May 28

You have created a lot of movement this month: some was intentional, some was karmic, and some was destiny. There are always going to be multiple layers to movement you create and experience. Karmic movement is the result of your intentions, feelings, and thoughts. Movement via destiny in this case means being exactly where you are meant to be, regardless of what you do or how much you wish you were somewhere else. Most of the time, these layers combine and steer our lives in the same direction. Other times they do not, which is where resistance and doubt tend to creep in. Today, be on the lookout for these points of resistance. See if you can identify what is causing friction, and allow yourself to be open to the angels creating a solution for you. The solution might be as simple as taking a breath and gently dropping back in to alignment with your day. Ask, receive, flow.

May 29

The manner in which you move through your day will show you what your mind is hooked to when you wake up. If you wake up and have good, positive thoughts, your day may be running smoothly. If, however, you wake up to your brain counting the ways everything could go wrong after a night of tossing and turning due to stress dreams, there is a good chance your day is not exactly flowing. The good news is that you can catch yourself in the morning and redirect or amplify your thoughts and the energy. Just as easily as you can see the pattern in your day, choosing to act or react differently changes the direction and shape your day will take. You can then enjoy and celebrate the direction of movement in your daily life. Identify, decide, flow.

May 30

The fantastic thing about knowledge is that once you know, you can't *not* know. Throughout this month, you have learned many different ways to move: when to slow down and rest, and when to speed up and create massive amounts of momentum. Your angel Daniel has guided and instructed you. Your tools have multiplied, your experience has increased, and your knowledge is creating movement and momentum all by itself. If you do find yourself stuck, stagnating, or out of flow, you know that you are the reason and are actively choosing to stay in the energy you have created. The downside to knowing is that inaction and resistance will be amplified and feel worse than ever before. Be mindful of the fact that having knowledge of movement means that your conscious mind can't unlearn how to do it.

May 31

You have come to the end of your journey with Daniel, at least for this cycle. Your journey can continue outside these pages, if you so choose. But as with all journeys that come to an end, it is important to see where you are and how far you have come. When you look back at the beginning of this month, can you see where you started? Track the journey Daniel has taken you on and give thanks to it. Even if the distance you traveled together looks small, its effects are vast. Honor all you have shifted, moved, and aligned to over the month, and give yourself a pat on the back. No matter where you now stand, you are not the same person you were when you started. Something in you has changed and will never go back to the way it was. Spend today honoring this new part of yourself and giving thanks to the you who had to be released in order for this new you to grow.

Closing Ceremony for the Month

Your time with angel Daniel has now come to an end, for this year anyway. It is time to pack up your altar for the angel of movement. It is important to give your altar a good cleaning as a way of closing the energy you have been working with over the past month. Wash your magical items, wipe down your altar's surface, and put any cards or images away. Remember, also, to wave a smoking herb bundle over the space so that you can cleanse the energy and reset it, making it ready for the next angel. As you clean and reset your altar, say a small prayer of thanks:

> *Angel Daniel, I thank thee*
> *For moving me this month*
> *For correcting my course*
> *For nudging me*
> *For showing me how to flow, flex, and focus*
> *With each move of my feet*

My life moves and shifts to a new beat
One created with you
I clean and clear this sacred workspace
This altar I cleanse
To honor you
To honor the work we have done.
Thank you.

Chapter Seven
JUNE

The Angel of Transmutation

Welcome to June, the month of transmutation. This month we are taking all the energy, opportunities, and possibilities that have flowed to us this year and refining them through the art of transmutation. Here, we make changes and tweaks to what we are creating so we can get into a more feeling-based vibration. The better we get at transmutation, the more peace, ease, and flow we can bring into our lives. Honestly I had no idea how important transmutation energy was until I personally started working with the angels in a deeper, more devotional way. I knew when the angels and I sat down to write this book that transmutation would be included. Throughout this month, your angel will give lessons, messages, and guidance around transmutation that could take the form of instructional tasks to ground the lesson. The meditations, observations, and guidance itself may sometimes be more abstract, as it is channeled material. Just know that whatever you personally receive from the daily prompt is correct and valid. It is not an accident that we are exploring this theme in a month that is transformative itself. In the Northern Hemisphere, summer is birthed in June and in the Southern Hemisphere, winter begins. Solstice season is upon us and brings with it the energy of transmutation. For this reason, we are working in sync with the natural magic of our planet this month. Whatever you bring forth to work on this month will have a cyclic nature to it. This is the season to heal, clear, and transmute. So relax into this month—you are perfectly aligned and everything is exactly how it is meant to be.

Connection Prayer: Bringing in the Energy of the Angel of Transmutation

To get the most out of your month with the angel Nel, set up your June altar. Once you have your altar cleansed and set up, light your candle. I recommend using indigo-colored candles for this month, as indigo is the color of projection, change, and transmutation. If you cannot find them, white is fine as it can represent any color we want. I highly recommend writing keywords on your candle about something you wish to transmute this month. It could be chaos to calm, feeling overwhelmed to peace, loss to profit. Just don't make your statement too long—you need to fit it on your candle, after all. When you are ready to light your candle, say the following prayer to bring in the energy of angel Nel and connect her to your June:

Angel Nel, I summon thee;
Change me
Not because I have to
Because I need to
The growth I have done
The life I am crafting
Requires me to change along with it
Transmute what is already inside of me
Free it
Help me find release
I bind you to this month of June on my calendar
We are in this together
A journey of two
One physical
One vibrational
All that was will be used
To bring about something new
A me of truth
My soul being

As it is said
So it is done
For now this change has begun.

Messages for the Days of the Month

June 1

The angels know that when you decide you want to make a change in your life, for the most part you are talking about surface-level changes to be more able to fit in or be accepted. In other words, you want to change for ego-based reasons. But when you decide to transmute who you are, you are committing to deep and profound change in the very energetic structure of your identity. This change happens on the level of the soul and comes from a place not ruled by the ego. Instead, your inner soul star sheds layers of your burned-through karma to create a new version of yourself. Your angel of the month wants to remind you that this work is not simple, nor is it quick. However, it is something all humans undertake at some point in their physical incarnations. You could even say that the entire human experience is an act of transmutation. This month, your angel Nel will teach you more about why this is so and how you can be an active rather than passive participant in your own transmutation process.

June 2

Can you identify the last time you felt like a new person, where the world around you looked new, fresh, and full of wonder? For some, this won't be too long ago as you are constantly in a cycle of transmutation, recreating yourself again and again. Others may struggle to remember the last time they allowed themselves to change, shift, and renew their concept of the self. Your angel Nel encourages you to think about today as a day of new possibilities, a day where all things can be seen with fresh eyes, a clear mind, and an open heart. Do not move through your day as you did yesterday. Find different approaches, new angles, and new solutions. Your angel wants you to get creative and make a list of new ways to approach old problems. Head into your day with confidence and clarity.

June 3

It's not often humans think about the messy part of change, possibly due to the low-level trauma experienced in the past as a result of change at some point in your short incarnations. You humans in general only want the result. The bad news is that you can't have results without the messy stage of pulling everything apart and putting it back together. The caterpillar goes through transmutation inside its cocoon—every part of what that caterpillar was is changed. It has to— otherwise there would be no butterfly. The good news is that you have a certain amount of control over how messy it has to be. The more detailed you are about what you will do, receive, and let go of in your cocoon, the less surprised and unprepared you will be. Today, plan your cocoon experience in detail. Maybe you want to start by wearing comfier pants. Or maybe you can schedule in more self-care days or end situations that you know will be toxic to your transformation process. Don't leave a single thing out.

June 4

Let's talk about time. Although it may be an illusion in the grander scheme of the universe, it is very real to you and me. Time is how you measure your journey and all the stops along the way. Your transmutation adventure needs a time frame. You will need to know exactly how long to prepare before entering your cocoon. You will also want to know how long to stay in the cocoon and at what point you will emerge and commit to show up and engage in the world as this new version of yourself. In other words, you need to add these event points to a calendar. Your angel recommends not drawing out any part of this journey, yet also giving things enough time to be done correctly and completely. Marking your transmutation on your calendar is a commitment and claims it as something important. So what are you waiting for? Go!

June 5

Let the preparations begin. Now that you have scheduled your transmutation journey on your calendar, it is time to consider all the things that need to be done before you enter your cocoon stage. A caterpillar isn't simply born and then immediately transmutates. There is time for the caterpillar to just be a caterpillar, to enjoy the journey, no matter how brief. During that time all the caterpillar does is prepare its body and mind for what will come next. You are now at that stage. Your angel says you must prepare and pay special attention to your mind, your only companion once you enter the cocoon stage of your journey. Preparation might mean getting some support, though the type greatly depends on the transmutation journey you are taking. Maybe it is enlisting the assistance of your ride-or-die BFF, or setting up regular meditation sessions. It could even be checking in with your angel at the end of each day to see how things are progressing. Just make sure whatever support you choose is right for the journey you are about to undertake.

June 6

It is time to consider putting your transmutation team into place. You will need help and assistance as you go through this process, little one. We do not recommend ever taking a journey like this alone. Grab a pen and paper and start thinking about who you would like to have on your team. Who will be your go-to person to talk out any and all hard emotions? Who will be your mindset maven who helps you keep your head on straight as you start to change your internal narrative? Also think about who or what will serve as your physical outlet. Remember that your team needs to cover your mental, emotional, and physical parts—all three are about to change. Perhaps now is a good time to start a yoga practice or get that gym membership. Perhaps joining a team sport is more your thing. Consider getting a mindset coach or even a life coach to help with other parts of your transmutation journey. The better-skilled your team, the better your transmutation journey will be.

June 7

As with all things that change, you may notice an element of fear about whether or not the deep change you are embarking upon this month will be the correct choice. It is normal to question, it is human to second-guess. It is our job as your guardian angels to remind you that everything you desire lives on the other side of your fear. This does not mean that fear disappears completely—it just means that those who walk through the barrier that separates themselves from their fear end up being happier than those who allow it to separate them from their heart's desires. In many respects, you must become one with your fear because in reality your fear *is* you, not something outside of you. Fear is a vibrational energy that lets you know when things in your life are moving, changing, and shifting. It is a natural part of you, so move toward it and see for yourself that this journey is the correct one for you at this time.

June 8

Nourishment is important in all stages of change, especially when that change is deep and profound. Today you and your angel will focus on how you are nourishing your body and how you are preparing it for the change you are creating. Remember that this change isn't superficial like changing your clothes—it is happening on an inner level. You are connecting to new parts of yourself and bringing them forward. These efforts will take a toll on your physical body, so nourishment is key. Today, focus on what you eat and how it makes your body feel. See if what you are eating is making you feel energized, alert, focused, and comfortable in your skin. Start eliminating foods that make you feel sleepy, bloated, foggy, or sluggish; they will not sustain you through your journey this month.

June 9

When going through transmutation, we do not just nourish our body—we must also nourish our minds. What you think, listen to, and read all feed your brain and, as with food, some are better for you than others. Remember also that what nourishes you may not nourish someone else. Today, focus on yourself and your own goals. Start curating information you find helpful, joyful, inspiring, and motivating. It needs to be relevant to the change you are making, and it needs to uplift you in a way that will keep you moving forward. Much like your body, your mind will focus better if the food you feed it is nutritious and not junk. A tired and worn-out mind creates tired and worn-out and overwhelming narratives that deplete the body of energy. An inspired, creative, curious mind is sparked with energy and lights up the body, making it ready for action. Feed your mind well today and you will reap the reward tomorrow.

June 10

The last part of you that needs to be taken care of for your journey is your spirit. Nel, your angel of the month, is here to assist you in that area, more than happy to point you in the right direction to meditations, chants, mudras, and prayers that will keep the vibrational part of yourself feeling uplifted, connected, and light. Sometimes it might be as simple as finding the right song or creating and curating a playlist to listen to throughout your transmutation process. Humans have turned to sound to feed their spirits for as long as they have acknowledged having one. From sitting among the trees listening to the forest, hearing waves crash onto the beach, or being moved by the voices of angels, sound has always fed and restored the spirit. Now you are being asked to find what will feed yours.

CHECK-IN ONE

It has now been ten days since you started working with the angel Nel and the theme of transmutation. Now is the ideal time to visit your altar and consider if the items on it are still relevant or if you need to switch them out or add to them. It is also time to give your altar space a bit of a clean, freshen up any cut flowers, and light your candles once more. Say a small prayer or mantra, or sit in silent meditation for a couple of minutes. This small journey to your altar will bring your mind, body, and soul back to a place of devotion and recenter you in the month's theme.

June 11

Transmutation is an inside job. However, the results will be seen outside of you in the world where you play, dance, and thrive. More than likely, your physical body will change as well. Even now, as you enter into the middle part of your journey, you might be noticing small changes. Perhaps you are doing your hair differently. Maybe you have started taking a different route to work. Or maybe you have started doing an activity that you have never done before. These are all exterior results of the change happening within you. Today, raise your awareness and see if you can find any other small yet significant shifts to your daily habits, the colors of clothing you wear, and even the food you decide to eat. These things may seem inconsequential until you understand that they are the result of all your hard work, showing you in real time that it's all coming together.

June 12

When you are faced with any sort of change, you will act in one of two ways from instinct: deny and dig in, or jump in with both feet and worry about the details later. There is a third option that, while not instinctual, is something some people learn over the course of their life—to pause, reflect, and do nothing but observe. Today you are being asked to select option three. This option offers you the very unique advantage of perspective. When we observe, we can make better decisions. And the further in to the transmutation process you get, the more important it becomes to make wiser, more intentional decisions. Watching how the energy of change moves, ripples, and expands is important to understanding how to navigate the new landscape change brings. So grab a notebook and a pen, because today you are making notes on what direction you wish to head next.

June 13

Your transmutation journey is really all about sculpting and molding the reality you wish to experience. For the most part, it is an individual journey, as you are crafting the person you wish to be. But it is also a community journey, as the person you create needs to be able to work, love, play, and live in the community surrounding them. Keep in mind that you are not being asked to limit yourself in any way to fit in. It is important, however, to remember that you might need to explore your current community further than you have before. The new you may not fit into the world of the old you. Your angel knows that the person you are becoming may need different experiences and environments in which they may thrive. As you slowly but surely carve out the new you, you are also sculpting the community you wish to be in. The more you refine yourself, the better you will get at finding the people, groups, and organizations that fit your new experience.

June 14

The best part of the transmutation process is molding a new you. First you create this new version of yourself with your mind and see your new self in all its glory. Then you tap into how this new version of you will feel as it moves through life. At this point, you will merge your thoughts and feelings to solidify the transmutation process. Last but not least, you will begin to embody this new version of yourself. Identify where you are in this process today. Your angel says that if you are still holding on to the old self, then you might be feeling angry and confused. If you are mid-process, you might be noticing how you pause more between thoughts, feelings, and actions. If you are further along, you may even start to see physical things change in your daily world while you remain peaceful, calm, and a sense of power washes over you.

June 15

When change becomes necessary, it is not just that we wish to do things differently, but that adaptation creates a totally different path to walk. When necessity bears down on us, we know for sure that an old cycle or old way of doing and being has come to a natural end, which is normal because all things eventually run their course. When this happens, a new branch of your path opens up and awaits you to make the necessary changes in order to walk it. Today, one of the branches is opening up. Something in your life has come to a completion and is requiring you to change, transmute, and adapt. This new branch should not be difficult to locate, as it will be surrounded by dead ends, closed doors, and stop signs. It will block you from going backward and only offer one clear path to move along.

June 16

Once you are well into the cycle of transmutation, you might notice that it starts to feel as though nothing is happening. Everywhere around you, others are hitting new milestones and finding joy while you seem to be standing still. This happens when you hit the middle of your transmutation process and is where you need to strengthen your emotional and mental body. On this part of the journey, you can speed things up ... or get offtrack completely. Today, your angel is asking you to keep your mind on the end result. Sit and visualize how you want to appear once this process is completed. Allow yourself to sink deep into your imagination and play. Do this a couple of times throughout your day for only a couple of minutes each time to keep you on track and in the zone of your transmutation energy.

June 17

The middle of any journey can be tough, and here in the deep transformational waters of transmutation, it is even more difficult than normal because the change you are going through is internal. Others will not notice that change right away, and there won't be too many outward indications that things are moving along. In this phase of your journey, faith is required. You are being asked to trust that things are moving the way they are supposed to and that you are getting closer to your end result even if it doesn't feel that way. You must also have faith in your angel to navigate you through this tricky phase of your journey. Just know that although it might feel like things have halted today, trust that they have not. Have faith that your angel is instead clearing, healing, and cleaning up the old self in order to birth the new. Trust this to be true and allow yourself to slowly keep moving forward.

June 18

There comes a point in all journeys where you have to surrender, let go, and step out of the way. Today is one of those days. No matter where you turn today, you will find that you have to step back, release your grip, relax into the moment, and trust that what is happening is a direct result of your transmutation process. Your angel knows that sometimes surrender can feel like giving up, giving in, and handing over your power. Yet this is not a time to feel defeated. Your angel wants you to instead see that allowing the universe to move all the pieces for you is the most powerful thing you can do. Knowing that others can see things you cannot is a courageous step toward making sure you get what you want. Lastly, there is a big difference between giving up following the limitations of the ego and choosing to trust an unlimited higher power. Close your eyes, take a deep breath, and let the word "release" be your guiding mantra for the day.

June 19

Today you need to reconnect to the emotional energy surrounding your end result. Why did you begin this journey of transmutation in the first place? Dig deeply into the emotions you have created around your reason and allow them to anchor you to the path you are currently walking. Your emotions are the only thing that will see you through as you control your thoughts, actions, and reactions. Today, open up and connect to the deeper part of you who is committed to change.

June 20

Today your angel wants you to see if you feel or think differently about your current relationships, especially when you consider where you are on your transmutation journey. Perhaps people who once gave you a sense of comfort no longer soothe you. Or maybe you have noticed that you are starting to enjoy the company of different people at your job. It is important to understand that as you move through this inner change, you will shift your relationships. This is neither good nor bad, just a natural evolution in who you are and whom you wish to engage with. There will be people in your circle who don't feel like a good match anymore, and this is okay. The angels ask that you do your reevaluation with love, compassion, and kindness for yourself and those who may no longer be able to sustain and maintain their relationship with you.

CHECK-IN TWO

You have now had twenty days working with your theme of transmutation and your angel Nel. It is time to pull out your journal and see how the prompts have been helping you stay in the energy of change and transformation. Starting with the following sentence, make lists of tangible results or situations in which your angel's assistance has aided you: "So far this month, I have_____." Once you are done, move on to the remainder of the month.

June 21

As you get deeper and deeper into your transmutation journey, you may start to feel like you have transmutation superpowers. This happens when you notice the energy of a room changes or shifts for the better the moment you walk into it. You might also start to notice that you are able to transmute others' anger and send them kindness and compassion. You may even start to see how your very presence can clean up a space just by being in it. This is the true power of change. When you are doing inner work, your outer world will start bending to your vibration. So be on the lookout today for examples of your new superpowers. The more you deepen your transmutation work, the cleaner the outer space around you becomes.

June 22

When the caterpillar realizes it no longer looks or feels the same, it must come to terms with how it will engage with the world around it. Before it emerges from the cocoon in its new butterfly body, there is a transition period that requires the caterpillar to let the old identity go once and for all so that it may embrace its new self. Today is your day to start embracing this new self. You are different than before. You are having different thoughts, feelings, and possibly even different desires. The way you look at the world has changed, and there is no going back to the old way of being. You might be feeling a sense of loss or grief. Your angel wants you to lean into that feeling, sink deeply into it, and let it wash over you so it can move on and out before you contemplate your own emerging ceremony.

June 23

As you get closer and closer to your emerging date, you might start to feel uncomfortable, as though life is tight. Situations might be making you uncomfortable and daily tasks could irritate you more than normal. You might even find yourself a little on the snappy side. Just know that this is completely normal, and these are all symptoms of a breakthrough or—more to the point—the coming breakthrough. Just as a growing embryo eventually runs out of room and needs to be birthed, your new self could start to find itself constricted in the cocoon that has been keeping it safe. Over the next few days, you are going to have to learn to soothe this feeling. Your angel suggests being kind to yourself. Use kind words when talking about yourself. Remember to always pause and take a breath before you respond to others. Over the next few days, mindfulness is going to be the name of the game.

June 24

The pressure you are feeling today is an indication that your transmutation process is drawing to an end. That which was once safe and cozy is now restrictive and uncomfortable. Remember this feeling—your angel knows what a great sign it will be in the future that you have outgrown people, places, and things. As the end draws closer, the pressure around you intensifies. The good news is that it's almost over. Truly, you are so close to the finish line. You have done so well and only good things await you on the other side of how you currently feel. It may not be the comfort you are looking for, but sometimes knowing that a situation is only temporary can give you the last bits of strength required to see it all through. Know that your entire angel team stands with you today, doing their best to make this final transition as easy as possible.

June 25

Moving might feel impossible today. Every turn you make feels as though it might break you as your cocoon gets ready to crack open. You may need to slow down, so take all the time you need to get through your daily tasks. Wherever possible, stop, breathe, and give your body a rest. Even a two-minute break to close your eyes and breathe in between tasks can help. Your transmutation process is ending, and the new you is birthing. The moment is now. Give yourself the space and time you need to move through these contractions. Remember that this process has a rhythm all its own, and your angel is right there with you helping you find the flow of this energy. You have done such an incredible job; this is it, your final push.

June 26

There is an intense and pleasurable feeling to freedom. You might almost feel dizzy with the life force energy that comes rushing toward you now that you have emerged from your transmutation cocoon. Just be mindful that this sudden rush of adrenaline won't last—eventually you will need to rest, restore, and give your body and mind time to recover from the emergence process of the last few days. You worked hard and used a lot of energy—now it needs to replenish. Today, allow yourself to seek out things that bring you comfort. It might be people, food, things, or even places. Just know that what once worked more than likely won't now. Be prepared to find new comforts and new ways to soothe the new you who has been birthed into the world.

June 27

Now that your time inside the transmutation cocoon has come to an end, you may find yourself in relearning phases. They won't last long, but they might be just long enough to cause you a level of unwanted frustration. It is important to understand that you can't skip this step; you must engage with it and be as patient as you can be. Your angels completely understand how irritating it can be to do a task or approach a situation as you always have, only to see everything fall flat. But remember that this is why you entered into the cocoon to begin with—to stop doing things in the same way you have always done them. Remind yourself today of why you took this journey to begin with, as your reason will get you through the nuances of learning how to move through your life as this new version of yourself.

June 28

Today, your angel is asking you to step into the vibrational energy of appreciation. It is time to acknowledge the people who have supported you on this journey: who showed up, stepped up, and listened to you as you changed, expanded, and moved through some intense growing pains? Go on your appreciation rants in a personal way: call them, take them out for a meal, and interact in a way that makes them feel like a VIP. No one is an island, and you would not be where you are today if someone, somewhere, didn't believe in you. Want to go the extra mile and earn some appreciation karma? Get these people a heart-centered gift, or write them a heartfelt card or letter of appreciation. Today is not about you—it is about all those people who showed you kindness along the path.

June 29

As you come to the end of your month of transmutation, it is important to take a moment and consider what comes next. Once you have relearned how to navigate your life again and figured out what your new superpowers are, think about what this means for the here and now. What will you do with this new you and the new energy you are emitting? One of the biggest missed opportunities for people who go through massive transformation is not grounding themselves in the present moment or allowing themselves to settle into this newness. Most people jump from one thing to the next. But not you, right? You want to make the lessons stick and make all the pain count. Make sure your sacrifice is worth it. This type of thinking is part of your new, expanded awareness. You could say that the transmutation process has upgraded your personal consciousness. Use it carefully, intentionally, and with purpose.

June 30

Well done—you made it to the end of the month! It might feel as though you moved mountains these past thirty days. You might still be feeling a little hungover after all of your accomplishments. But you also know that everything—every step, piece of resistance, breakdown that turned into a magical breakthrough—was all worth it. So raise a glass of any kind of beverage and claim your victory. The angels stand around you today and celebrate in your honor. They are holding a cosmic party just for you, so step into the celebratory vibes of completion.

Closing Ceremony for the Month

Your time with angel Nel has now come to an end, for this year anyway. It is time to pack up your altar for the angel of transmutation. There may be other things that were part of your cocoon (but not part of your altar) that may need to be packed up as well. It is important to give your altar and other spaces you may have used during your transmutation process a good cleaning to cleanse the energy you have been working with over the past month. Wash your magical items, wipe down your altar's surface, and put any cards or images away. Remember to wave a smoking herb bundle over the space, so that you can cleanse the energy, reset it, and prepare it for the next angel. As you clean and reset your altar, say a small prayer of thanks:

> *Angel Nel, I thank thee*
> *For holding sacred space*
> *For keeping me safe*
> *For protecting me*
> *For showing me how to change, transform, and transmute*

With each wiggle of my body
My energy has become something new
One created with you
I clean and clear this sacred workspace
This altar I cleanse
To honor you
To honor the work we have done.
Thank you.

Chapter Eight

JULY

Penne

The Angel of Play

Welcome to July, the month of play. I have a secret to share: this is my birthday month! Yay, me. Not that I actually celebrate my birthday; acknowledging I am one foot closer to the grave seems depressing to me. However, the energy of this month always feels playful. Because I was born in the Southern Hemisphere, that makes me a mid-winter baby. Yet here in the Northern Hemisphere, where I live now, it is mid-summer. The weather makes it a little harder for me to play, because it's usually 115° here in the desert on my birthday. There's no dip in the energy, however—I still feel the nudges of fun and can hear the giggle of my angels. I want to share all of that lovely energy with you, and luckily for us, angel Penne is with us for the entire month. Throughout this month your angel will give you lessons, messages, and guidance related to play that could take the form of instructional tasks to ground the lesson. The meditations, observations, and guidance itself may sometimes be more abstract, as it is channeled material. Just know that whatever you personally receive from the daily prompt is correct and valid. Considering all the growth, change, and shifting you have done over the last six months, you deserve a whole month of play, regardless of the season this month falls in for you.

Connection Prayer: Bringing in the Energy of the Angel of Play

To get the most out of your month with the angel Penne, set up your July altar and make sure it is fun and playful. Keep the items on your altar for this month whimsical and filled with the energy of play. I also recommend leaving space on your altar to add things to it as you move through the month, especially if you go somewhere fun to play and want to add your admission ticket or a photo of yourself playing! Once your altar is cleansed and set up, light your candle. I recommend using pink candles this month, as they represent heart energy. Play is all about opening the heart and allowing yourself to surrender to fun, but if you cannot find pink candles, white is fine, as it can represent any color we want. Write keywords on your candles that indicate whatever you consider play: reading, painting, skating, hiking, fishing, golf, tennis, video games, and so on. When you are ready to light your candle, say the following prayer to bring in the energy of angel Penne and connect her to your July.

Angel Penne, I summon thee;
For it is time
To come and play with me
This month we will share
Imagination
Inspiration
Laughter
And fun
I am ready
To learn anew
All your gifts and games
Let's throw out all the rules
Make it up as we go along
I bind you to this month of June on my calendar
We are in this together
For this play date
Has begun.

Messages for the Days of the Month
July 1

Play is an essential part of human creativity. It swirls inside of you no matter your age. It is that part of you that wants to lay down all the weight of responsibility just for a moment to do something that feels fun instead. Play connects you to the life force energy that runs through your physical body, and the more you play, the more energy you spark. Yet whatever is play to you may not be play to someone else. This month, you are going to find out what play means to you on a soul level. What sort of activities spark you will be as unique as you are—which, as the angels know, is the entire point. When you attune to the energy that lights you up, your unique light will glow stronger than ever before.

July 2

Did you know that just fifteen minutes of play a day can change your energy, mindset, and productivity? Today you are being asked by your angel Penne to schedule in fifteen minutes of active playtime. Set an alarm and make sure you complete the task. Play is going to look different for everyone, so make sure it is authentic to you and fits your definition of play. As long as your activity connects you to your imagination and gets you out of your problem-focused mind, you will see how incredible the rest of your day will be. Once you have completed your playdate with yourself, schedule this fifteen-minute slot into every day on your calendar.

July 3

Play can sometimes feel like a celebration, and that's because their frequencies are very similar. Angel Penne says that there are times where you end up merging the two frequencies and create a massive current of creative magic. With this in mind, look at ways you can combine play and celebration today. Know that neither of these things needs to be large in scale or take up a lot of time. You already have your fifteen minutes of playtime scheduled, so it's not as though you need to carve out extra time for this step. All you have to do is find something to celebrate during your playtime. Who knows, maybe you will celebrate simply being able to keep your play date. Don't overthink—just let whatever first comes to mind be the thing you celebrate today.

July 4

Your angel sees play as the spark that ignites the wheel of joy. Today, look for ways to bring more playful moments into your mundane tasks. It could be singing while you work, dancing in your seat as you make your way through your never-ending to-do list, or even laughing and joking with those around you during moments of transition throughout your day. Think of this as your play habit stack routine. When faced with a mundane task, stack it with a form of play and before you know it, your life will be filled with moments that keep the joy wheel turning.

July 5

Today your task is to strategically and actively bring play into other people's lives. Play is much more fun when done with others. The more joy we spark, the happier we all feel. And let's face it: laughter is contagious. If you are feeling up to it, your mission is to set a target and aim your playful energy at those around you. Make sure you are doing it in a caring, kind, and compassionate manner; we do not want others to link the act of play with obnoxious behavior. Start small and work your way up with your playful energy. Respect others' boundaries and do your best to be aware when you know you have reached someone else's limits. Play is a great way to get to know someone, so use this opportunity to learn something new about the people around you that perhaps you wouldn't have known if hadn't actively sought them out as playmates for the day.

July 6

Play can be infectious. Once you start amping up your own personal joy, those around you may also want some of what you have. They may want to know why you seem less stressed and more connected than you were before. Share with them, and give others the opportunity to bring more play into their lives. The more we can connect, enhance, and engage with the energy of play, the more we as a community can increase our levels of kindness, empathy, and compassion. Today, share your play secrets. Speak to others about the benefits and transformations you have seen and experienced since bringing a little more play into your life. Explain why this has been important for you and how you can see it helping them if they choose to add more play to their lives. Your story of play and joy may be the very things someone else needs to hear today to turn their life around.

July 7

People often think of play as something that is physical, loud, and possibly even childish. While none of these are discouraged, it is important to know that play can be quiet, gentle, and look like very serious "grown-up" activities. Play is nothing more than allowing yourself space and opportunity to let your imagination run wild: it could happen in a silent, still manner just as easily as it could explode out of you in a fit of laughter. Today, your angel would like you to explore some of these quieter ways to play. See if you can find a deeper way to connect with your imagination that doesn't require physical effort. It might be as simple as allowing yourself to daydream for ten minutes or journaling, painting, looking at picture books, visiting an art gallery, or finding a nice seat and watching the trees outside your window dance in the wind. These are all moments of play. They will all create the same sense of calm and joy. Find one that resonates with you and enjoy your playtime today.

July 8

Today your angel is asking you to think about how you can bring the element of play into problem solving. You see, not all solutions come from a logical mind. Oftentimes they require a creative, imaginative, curious mind, which is where the flow of the solution resides. By introducing the energy of play to a problem today, you will very likely discharge the tension you have been feeling around it. Oftentimes we put a lot of pressure on ourselves to get something done right. But with the energy of play in your problem-solving tool kit, you can relax into the solution and let your imagination do all the heavy lifting. Perhaps the problem you will need to solve today will involve other people and you'll be able to teach them a new way of dealing with a problem they may also have been thinking about or that was causing them stress.

July 9

Your angel wants you to think about how you can bring the element of play into your health today. For the most part, we take our health quite seriously. There will be times where you think about your body and physical experience in a somber and worrisome manner. This adds stress to your immune system and tends to weigh you and your body down, making you feel heavy, tired, and unable to focus for long periods of time. When you bring in the energy of play you lighten the load on your body. You start to unclench your jaw and loosen your neck and shoulders. A small amount of play in your health and well-being regimen will assist in lowering your overall stress and might even bring you more joy, which has been known to strengthen the immune system. Making play a part of a healthy lifestyle will only add more benefits to your life.

July 10

If you have children or have had a child in your life, you will know that one of the best ways to get them to engage with their food is through the act of play. You do this through making their food fun and creating games to make the habit of eating fun. For whatever reason, we forget about the act of play when it comes to our food as adults. We stop making smiley-face pancakes and cater-pillar cucumbers and instead start thinking of food as either an enemy or a way of numbing our feelings. It's very easy for these attitudes to lead to unhealthy relationships with the fuel our bodies need to thrive and repair. Today your angel wants you to go back to playing with your food: be creative with how you arrange the food on your plate, and be more relaxed and mindful when you eat. Put a smile on your face from beginning to end and infuse your food with hap-piness and imagination.

CHECK-IN ONE

It has now been ten days since you started working with the angel Penne and the theme of play. Now is the ideal time to visit your altar and consider if the items you set it up with are still relevant or if you need to switch them out or add to them. It is also time to give your altar space a bit of a clean, freshen up any cut flowers, and light your candles once more. Say a small prayer or mantra, or sit in silent meditation for a couple of minutes. This small journey to your altar will bring your mind, body, and soul back to a place of devotion and center you in the month's theme.

July 11

Today, the angels ask you to identify an area of your life in which you have been struggling, a space in your day-to-day in which you know you could do better in but have yet to see any sort of improvement. The angels ask that, just for today, you turn that area of your life into a game. Make it playful and fun. One of the reasons this area of your life has been causing you so much tension is that when you approach it, you are filled with stress and anxiety. Let the angels flip that script for you: from now on, before moving your mind into this area of your life, take a deep breath and laugh. Laugh out loud and let the tension go. Then proceed to the task at hand with the intent of making it fun and playful. If you notice you have clenched your jaw or tightened your shoulders at any time, stop, breathe, and laugh again. The angels want you to drop the emotional charge around this area of your life, and it all starts today.

July 12

Today, the angels are asking you to see if you can identify when others are in the flow of play. Play is different for every person on the planet, so it is going to look unique between individuals. Part of your task is to find new and creative ways to expand your definition of play and maybe even ignite your creative self to add more types of play into your daily experience. To make sure you get a wide variety of play documented, consider seeing it from the perspective of age groups, workplaces, social spaces, groups, and individuals. Because play can be seasonal, take notice if something you are observing right now is only possible during summer in the Northern Hemisphere (or winter in the Southern Hemisphere). Sounds like you have a busy day—better get to it.

July 13

Sometimes, play looks an awful lot like rest, and you could be forgiven for confusing the two. Oftentimes when you need to switch from life mode to play, your body slows down and you might even find yourself yawning a lot. In this state, you might find curling up with a good book, watching a movie, doing some baking, or snuggling on the couch with your pets or partner more appealing. This period of slow rest is vibrating on a similar frequency to play. So as you move through your tasks today, notice when your body starts to slow down—

this is a signal to rest, play, and shift your focus, even if for only fifteen minutes. You could discover that you've been playing this way for a while and never knew!

July 14

Today, your angel wants you to think about how you can turn the idea of money into a fun and exciting game. You might even consider opening an "angel account," (imaginary, of course). Every time you see a feather or coin on your path, imagine a hundred dollars being deposited into your angel account (again, not real money into a real bank account). Did you see four or five feathers in one day? Boom, that's four or five hundred dollars in your angel account. This way of playing with your money helps reset your thinking about how easy it is for money to be deposited into your account. If you make it a game and use your imagination, you can let go of stress you have around money and reprogram your mind to attract money into your bank every time you see a feather or coin on the street. What an exciting experiment to start today.

July 15

Today is fun-with-your-body day! For the most part, humans take their bodies way too seriously, always concerned about the shape, size, and various parts when really, bodies are nothing more than vehicles to carry your souls around so that they can have a physical experience. Instead of worrying about all your parts and whether they are the right shape and size, have fun with your body. Paint it. Dress it in funny, bright colors. Decorate it, pamper it, rest it. Just for today, take the weight of expectation off it. Let your body be exactly how it is and enjoy all the things it can do, see, touch, taste, and smell. How fun is it to taste something new? How exciting is it to see something magical happen before your very eyes? How moving is it to hear a piece of music that vibrates deep in your soul? This is your body at play. This is your body doing exactly what it was created to do.

July 16

Today is play-with-your-house day. Yes, today the angels want you to keep this energy of play running through your life and bring it to your house. How can you dress up your house and make it feel like a playtime pal? This might involve adding some new curtains, adding fun art to the walls, or even just giving it a good tidy up. Setting the energy of your house to play will only assist you to keep this energy in your electromagnetic field. The more you vibrate the energy of play, the more effective this whole play thing will be. So roll up your sleeves and don't forget to smile, because today you are going to set about playing with your house and making your living space more joyful, light, and fun.

July 17

Today your angel wants you to play in the dirt: get your hands dirty and feel connected to something that is living but is not human. This play can be done in the comfort of your own garden or even with your indoor plants. Gardeners don't really need to be told to go play in the dirt because they already know how healing and beneficial this form of play is to the mind, body, and soul. If you don't have even have one houseplant, today is the day to go get one. The very act of selecting a plant is play. Trusting yourself to keep something alive is a big leap, and this exercise might just be what you need to elevate your sense of self-trust. There are plenty of hardy plants out there, so don't be afraid to ask the nursery what they recommend for your situation. No matter if you are a plant lover or a plant beginner, today is your day to get the gardening gloves out and get your dirt on.

July 18

Today your angels want you to have fun with water. Water is an enormous part of life in the physical world, essential for growth for all beings. Incorporating water into your playtime is a good way to respect and honor it. Water play can be anything from a day at the beach, or collecting rocks by a river, to taking a hot bath, or making a nice cup of tea. The list of ways to bring water play into your daily life is endless. Perhaps you have wanted to bring a pond into your garden to encourage more wildlife into your ecosystem. Or maybe you have wanted to collect more rainwater and today is the day you finally get around to buying your rain barrel. It might even be that you want to celebrate the end of an incredible day with a small tea ceremony in which you infuse your cup with love and gratitude. It won't be hard to pick something today, so have fun and enjoy your water play.

July 19

For something completely different, today the angels would like you to play with your feet! Yes, you heard that correctly. Your feet are an important part of your body that not only hold you up but connect you to the physical realm. So today, honor your feet, the first vehicle you ever operated. You can play with your feet any way you want: get a pedicure or a foot massage. Find a nice cream to soothe them. Wear some fun and playful socks. Wiggle your toes or use them to paint with. Splash in some puddles. There really is an endless list of ways to bring more play to your feet. You might even consider walking barefoot and liberating your feet from your shoes. Feel the wind between your toes and give thanks for the way your feet support you each and every day of your life.

July 20

Today, it is time to play with your hands. Your hands do a lot for you—they hold things, feed you, help with transportation, and for some they are the very thing used to earn a living. Your hands work hard every day and have been doing so since you figured out you had them. Celebrate them and do something that honors their tireless efforts for making your life easier today. Get your hands massaged or go for a manicure. Perhaps find a nice hand cream to moisturize them, or consider getting some fun and fantastic gloves. Move your focus to your hands and see what magical fun you can have with them. They already do so much, so it is time to let them know you appreciate them and see them. Today, allow them some playtime.

CHECK-IN TWO

You have now had twenty days working with the theme of play and your angel Penne. It is time to pull out your journal and see how the prompts have been helping you stay playful. Start with the following prompt and make lists of tangible results or situations where your angel's assistance has aided you: "So far this month, I have_____."
Once you are done, move on to the remainder of the month.

July 21

It is easy to get far into your month and forget about the goals you set at the beginning. Today, your angel wants you to go back to revisit the list of goals you made at the start of the month, taking note of the one about factoring in fifteen minutes of play a day. Today, reevaluate to see whether you have been moving energy toward these tasks each day or if you have lost your focus and have been giving energy to something else. Use this little check-in to have some fun. Do not beat yourself up if you have strayed from your list. Instead, make a plan to have as much fun as possible to get back on track. Give yourself something fun, either as a reward if you have managed to stay on track, or not—the more fun you can make this task, the less guilt and shame you will feel around your journey toward your goals.

July 22

In the outside world we are bombarded with messages, words, noises, and all sorts of information. Today, take what you see around you and create funny stories with it or maybe a witty mantra. If you see a billboard advertisement, think of a fun way to play around with the words. Children naturally engage in this sort of word play and can make themselves laugh by adding sound effects. Now it's your turn: see the world outside you as nothing more than material for your own playful story. Perhaps your bus stop is actually the terminal to an intergalactic portal. Or your local cafe is really a hangout for pirates who pass messages by getting people's names wrong when writing them on their cups. The possibilities around you are endless. So go have fun today and create a world within the one you think you already know.

July 23

Today, find as many ways as possible to bring dance into your life. You can start by waving your arms, bobbing your head, or going all-out with your body and letting the beat move you. Sound is incredibly healing, and dance is a wonderful way to move energy through the body. This act of play is not only beneficial for your physical body but will help with your mental and emotional bodies as well. We angels love music, and grooving to a beat is a daily ritual of ours. Why do you think there are so many songs about us? Today, find your inner dancer and give them permission to come out and play. There is no wrong or right way to move your body and appreciate a beat. So drop your comparison and move your feet!

July 24

Your angel wants to remind you that play is sometimes a lot like prayer. A good prayer is like a love letter filled with words of thanks and praise for something yet to be fulfilled. When one prays for rain, one thanks the rain. When we pray for health, we thank our body for its health and well-being. This is a form of imagination that, in turn, serves as the key to play. So where can you pray today? What can you imagine already being done and for which you offer a love letter of heartfelt thanks? This form of play is more for the heart than the head, yet the mind also benefits greatly from this simple act. We, your everyday angels, pray to you, for opening space in your day to play with us and allowing us into your lives so we can create miracles for you on a daily basis.

July 25

This month, your angel has been showing you all the possible ways play can become a natural part of your day, in playing with your feet, moving your body, and finding creative ways to play with others. Some of those ways would have felt more aligned for you than others. Which ones have you really enjoyed? Which forms of play make you light up or calm down? The more you make play and its energy part of your life, the easier it will be to stay connected to imagination and inspiration. Your angel wants you to take a couple of minutes today to do a small review of all the ways you have included play in your life and start identifying the ones you know you will normalize and be sustainable long after this month is over.

July 26

For most of your adult life, you have normalized things that look a lot like work. They aren't habits created to bring you joy or even make you feel more connected to your body. Instead, they have normalized disconnection and feelings of hopelessness. Play, however, plugs you back into the energy of that which you call Source or god energy. This energy is effortless in its expression and sounds a lot like laughter. Although once a very normal part of your life until a certain age, you can still normalize play once again. This does not mean you won't take your responsibilities seriously or abandon all your structure and security. It does mean, however, that these things won't feel so heavy; life itself may feel less like a burden and more like a blessing. As you get closer to the end of this month, remember that once upon a time in your very own life, everything you have done this month was completely normal and can be once again.

July 27

As you get older, you need more things to keep up your cognitive skills. One of the best ways is through play. Even a couple of minutes a day (the angels of course recommend fifteen) can help keep your brain active and your creative mind engaged. Too often, our adult mind gets weighed down by stress and bombarded with things we feel we should be doing rather than taking time for things that help promote our overall health and well-being. Even playing games on your phone will be incredibly beneficial. Today, find a game that you enjoy and give your brain and creative mind a workout. There really is a game or form of play for every single person. The only limitation is your own personal beliefs around playtime.

July 28

Finding things to laugh at every day is good for the heart and mind. If you get nothing else from this chapter, let it be heart health, happiness, and finding things to laugh about. Although a good ol' belly laugh is preferred, a smirk or chuckle is more than adequate. Toddlers are forever telling themselves jokes no one else gets and laughing their little socks off, which is perfect energy for this chapter. Walk through your day and crack yourself up over and over again. No one else has to get the joke; all that matters is that you do. Find the funny in your day and your heart will thank you. Making play part of your new normal is really about keeping your mind and heart in a space of joyful coherence.

July 29

It is important to remember that play isn't just an action, nor is it something to mark off your daily to-do list. Your angel wants you to feel it as an energy that burns through your entire body and changes how you think and the emotions you vibrate. So even though you might have found yourself going through the playtime motions this month, it is crucial that you find a way to be in the energy of the play. Truly allow yourself to open up and feel fun, whimsy, and play from the top of your head to the tips of your toes. There are no downsides to embracing this feeling, only benefits. So relax, lean in, and allow the energy of play to wash over you today.

July 30

Sometimes play looks like everyday life. Over the last month, we have discussed various ways to bring in the energy of play through intention, though it is important to understand that everything about the human experience is playful. It is vital that you remember this, especially in moments where you don't feel as though you are in the energy of play. We do not equate play to fun, though it sure does amplify the energy of joy. Angels see play as the art of being, allowing you to be the vessel through which the energy of play will show up. On some days, that will look very different from fun. Today, allow yourself to relax and move through the playground of life just as you are.

July 31

Play doesn't only have to be something you do—it can be something you share or a space you can create where others can engage with it. Today, offer an invitation to someone close to you to play. Explain to them the benefits of taking a break in their day and help them give themselves permission to simply be. Oftentimes others around us are waiting for someone, anyone, to give them permission to drop their shoulders, unclench their jaws, and relax into silliness. We know that no one really needs to be "granted" space, but all adults carry the weight of responsibility with them. Today, be the person who offers the space to let go. Vibrate to the energy of play and offer its gifts to those who need it.

Closing Ceremony for the Month

Your time with angel Penne has now come to an end, for this year anyway. It is time to pack up your altar for the angel of play. Perhaps you bought some new toys, games, or sporting equipment this month. You might want to put it away, though your angel would love for you to keep it out and keep this practice in your life. It is important to give your altar and other spaces you may have used during your playtime a good cleaning as a way of closing the energy that you have been working with over the past month. Wash your magical items, wipe down your altar's surface, and put any cards or images away. Remember to also wave a smoking herb bundle over the space so that you can cleanse the energy and reset it, making it ready for the next angel. As you clean and reset your altar, say a small prayer of thanks:

Angel Penne, I thank thee
For coming and showing me
How to play
How to have fun
How to let go
How to feel more free
Thank you for giving me this gift
For teaching me how to share it with others
And how to hold space for play in my day
For now, I clean and clear this sacred workspace
This altar I cleanse
To honor you
To honor the work we have done.
Thank you.

Chapter Nine
AUGUST

Solis
The Angel of Passion

Welcome to August, the month of passion. In this chapter, you will learn about how the angels see the energy of passion. You may find that their perspective doesn't always align with what you were taught about passion, but Solis would like you to stay open and explore the possibilities over the next thirty days. Throughout this month, your angel will give you lessons, messages, and guidance around the energy of passion that could take the form of instructional tasks that ground the lesson. The meditations, observations, or the guidance itself may be more abstract, as the material is channeled. Just know that whatever you personally receive from the daily prompt is correct and valid. Passion is a very interesting energy that is not being used to its fullest potential. The angels hope that at the end of this month you will have a deeper understanding of passion and how to leverage it to create a day that flows and a life filled with more joy and less suffering. Really, all your angels want for you is precisely more love and joy, and less pain.

Connection Prayer: Bringing in
the Energy of the Angel of Passion

To get the most out of your month with the angel Solis, set up your August altar. It can include objects or pictures that currently ignite your passion energy. Everyone has different things that light them up and get them excited about life, so make this altar personal to you. Even if there is only one thing in your life right now that brings you any sort of joy, feature it on your altar. I also recommend leaving space on your altar to add things as you move through your month. Once your altar is cleansed and set up, light your candle. This month, I recommend using red candles, as they represent passion energy. If you cannot find red candles, white is fine, as it can represent any color we want. When you are ready to light your candle, say the following prayer to bring in the energy of angel Solis and connect them to your August.

Angel Solis, I summon thee;
Bring fire to my life
Excite me
Get me eager to dive into the day
Show me ways to increase my joy
Teach me how to move with confidence
Stir my emotions
Soothe my pain
Light me up
Like a divine flame
Together we will journey this month
As I bind you to my August calendar.
Sparks will fly
Laughter will reign
As energy flows
Through my day-to-day.
As it is said
With these words out loud
I open this adventure
It has begun.

Messages for the Days of the Month

August 1

Passion, like love, seems to lose a little bit of its true meaning when spoken about by humans. Although both are emotive by nature, neither love nor passion are biased or judgmental energy. Neither passion nor love come with a set of conditions or a checklist. Both are, however, forms of pure energy that only know how to flow to you, within you, and through you. Just like love, passion has an intensity to it that can and will move you, emotionally, mentally, and physically. When we angels talk about passion, we do not talk about it in the same way humans do. For that reason, we are structuring your monthly activities around reconnecting you to the source of true passion, the spark of inspiration that moves you so deeply and profoundly, already swirling inside you. Get ready, little one—this is going to be a very interesting month indeed.

August 2

Passion can often be disguised as what makes you smile. The upward turning of your lips is the physical manifestation of passion meeting your aura and moving through your body. It might even feel like a kiss from your angel. Today, be on the lookout for situations in which this feeling washes over you—it could be a person, situation, or even a luscious thought. Be mindful of the situations that create your gentle smile, and allow yourself to open up a little more to the energy of passion as it ripples through you and those around you.

August 3

There are moments that just stop you in your tracks and make your heart sing. They aren't overly big and it's often that your response can surprise even you. This is the essence of passion showing itself to you in the mundane corners of your life in those small, seemingly insignificant moments felt deep in your soul. For the most part, we just keep moving through these small moments when they appear, not really honoring the energy exchange. Today, your angel wants you to be ready to receive the blessing of these moments and acknowledge them when they happen. Let the essence of passion flow over you and spark new light codes within your vibrational body, while amping up the dopamine in your brain. These small moments are so good for your mental health that your angel is eager for you to embrace and leverage the hell out of them.

August 4

For the most part, we talk about passion as if it is something outside ourselves, something external that causes a response within us. Yet we want you to think about passion as an energy that can start and end within you, a light or spark for you as a soul. Know that your ability to be here in the dance of life is an expression of something that is manifesting inside of you through your passion for who you are and all you are capable of becoming, not responding to stimuli outside you. Today we ask you to turn inward. Close your eyes and block the world out for just a moment and connect with your heartbeat. Feel each beat as the drum of your soul's passion, the dance to which your life is choreographed, your soul flame. It is alive, excited, and full of energy.

August 5

Passion can feel a lot like connection, that spark where you immediately feel a sense of belonging in someone else's energy. Sometimes you meet people whom you just know are members of your soul family. The passion energy flares between you and there is an instant rapport. The great thing about this sort of connection is that it is usually spontaneous. It happened not because you set out to find it but because you were open and receptive to the energy of play and exploration. This is how the angels want you to move through your day today: open and receptive. Just see where you can notice the moment this connection energy shows up. Note, too, that not all of these connections are going to be long-term. In fact, most are short-term and could be mistakenly considered transactional. Do not confuse this kind of connection with making a new friend. That said, if the spark is bright enough, you never know where this passion energy will take you.

August 6

Spontaneous action is passion at its finest, when you are moved so completely by the energy of Spirit that you go without allowing the mind a chance to think about it. More often than not, your mind will interfere with wherever the angels wish to move you. The mind has a wonderful way of stopping you in your tracks and fizzing out the flow of passion energy. But Solis wants you to understand that passion will move you—it is direct guidance from the higher part of yourself to get you closer to your heart's desires. Passion is nothing more than soul alignment with what your divine self craves. So today, watch and see what you being moved toward … or what you are being moved away from. Make a mental list of people you seem to be guided to today as well as situations your angel seems to be keeping you away from. Today is a lesson in passion leading the flow of your day.

August 7

Passion isn't always joyful. For the most part, people think of passion as something positive and life-affirming. And while one side of passion certainly is, the other side … not so much. Solis wants to remind you that passion is a fire, and fire burns. It can get out of control and destroy. In and of itself, destruction is not a bad thing. Sometimes you need to tear things down and smash apart feelings, blocks, and situations. When done deliberately, this is your passion used in a healing action. Today, your angel wants you to be on the lookout for where your passion is perhaps igniting your world in a less-than-desirable way, causing conflict and rage instead of excitement and adventure. For now, don't judge it, just observe. This is a learning day, and you are only gathering information about how passion is moving through your life.

August 8

Have you ever wondered where that last little spark of energy comes from at the end of the workday, the last flash of energy that pulses through you and helps you get the last item on your list checked off or get through that last call or meeting of the day? That little spark is passion. It feels a lot like a microdose of motivation that urges you toward the finish line, and it cheers you on and gets you to do what feels impossible. It is the part of your higher self that wants to leave you feeling accomplished and clear so your slate is clean tomorrow. It is passion that prevents you from experiencing energy leaks and allows you to rest easy when you finally place your head on the pillow. It may not seem like a lot at the moment, but this tiny spark is a powerful form of passion. Notice it today when it appears and give it your thanks.

August 9

Passion can sometimes show up as frustration that happens when you feel you are lagging behind or things are taking too long to manifest. The energy of passion starts to bubble and boil inside of you and before you know it, you have become a little snippy, and your abrasive behavior can quickly turn to defeatism. Yet the only thing your passion was trying to tell you was that things are forming in their own time so that they can be perfect in every way. The ego wants everything right now, but the soul wants things when they are ready and in their most perfect form, delivered in the easiest way. Today, watch where you are allowing yourself to fixate on the timing of things. It may be your ego working hard to sabotage your soul's desires. Instead of feeding the frustration, thank it. Let it know that you are aware and things are taken care of. Then, move on with your day.

August 10

Passion can show up as a 3 a.m. wake-up call, energy that pulls you from your sleep and demands you get up and take action. As a writer, I know this call only too well. Ideas and sparks of inspiration burst me out of my slumber and need to be captured. But this sudden inspiration also happens when we are seeking an answer to a problem or a solution to a situation. Inspiration can come in hot and heavy in the twilight hours of the early morning. Think of it as is the Divine being passionate with you, burning through your subconscious straight into your conscious mind. It moves you out of bed and to your notebook, journal, or recording device. Sometimes we can fall back to sleep once inspiration has had its way with us, but other times we find ourselves so full of energy that we stay awake and ride the wave of the coming day. Consider both to be blessings, a communion with Spirit that is intimate, raw in its nature, and just for you.

CHECK-IN ONE

It has now been ten days since you began working with the angel Solis and the theme of passion. Now is the ideal time to visit your altar and consider if the items you set it up with are still relevant or if you need to switch them out or add to them. It is also time to give your altar space a bit of a clean, freshen up any cut flowers, and light your candles once more. Say a small prayer or mantra, or sit in silent meditation for a couple of minutes. This small journey to your altar will bring your mind, body, and soul back to a place of devotion and center you in the month's theme.

August 11

There will be times in your life (and today may be one of them) where you do not really feel all that passionate. You have no spark or zest for life and would prefer to spend your day hidden in a pillow fort with a pint of ice cream. For the most part, many believe this is the sort of day lacking in passion. But your angel says it is not. We have come to believe that if something is not driving us with intense urgency, we must be lacking the vibrational energy that passion can sometimes bring. The truth is that you are just as passionate about being left alone, having space, and eating ice cream as you are about the things that rev your engine. Today's angel message is that passion doesn't always look like a blazing inferno—it can look like pillow forts, cozy blankets, TV binging, and comfort food. Passion as an energy does not come and go. It merely shifts and molds itself around our desire for the day, whatever it may be and however it may look.

August 12

Passion can look a lot like sharing. There are times—and today may be one of them—where you get so excited about something that you feel you need to share it with everyone you come into contact with. It could be a new book, a new recipe, a new clothing store, or anything that moves you into a place of joy. There is a driving need for you to share this good feeling with as many people as possible. Often, passion comes alive when shared through joyful co-creation because sharing is a basic human instinct. Deep in your human programming, you really do want people around you to be happy. So today, your angel wants you to see where you can share in your day. This might be sharing wisdom, expertise, leaving a larger tip, or even offering a lift to a co-worker. All these small sharing moments fill your day with the energy of passion.

August 13

Newness is in the air today, mixed with the promise of something you have not experienced. The excitement, anticipation, and even the fear feel a lot like passion. When you do something you have never done before, there is a well of mixed emotions that swirl around you. There is a level of expectancy and a fair amount of hesitancy. This is passion in its very raw and wild form. The anticipation of new things feels like dancing on the edge of a blade: things could go very well and leave you feeling like you conquered the world. Or you could slip, cut yourself, and lick your wounds for days to come. You will never know which of these scenarios will happen unless you do it. It is the unpredictable nature of newness that stops many people from following the nudges of energy passion gives them. But not you, dear one—you like to live life on the edge; otherwise you would not hang out with angels! Today, look for new things. Lean into the wild, raw pulse of passion. Spread your wings and see what happens.

August 14

There will be days where passion looks a lot like running away into the hills, sometimes literally: Everyone needs a day off or a break from looking at screens, answering calls, dealing with people. You may very well get a nudge, call, or a pull to do anything other than more work. It is often good to follow those sparks of passion. For one, they often clean out stuck energy. They can do wonders for your mental health—not to mention they can improve your productivity. You would be surprised how much more efficient you can be after you have given yourself permission to step outside, unplug, and restore your natural battery. So, if it is safe to do so, run away today. Frolic, play, and see where the energy of passion will lead you.

August 15

As you enter the middle of the month, it is a good time to reflect on how and where passion has been showing up in your days. Over the last two weeks, you and your angel have explored various ways passion can and does make its way into your life. It could have been inspired action, attraction, play, taking a day off, or even learning how to control your inner fire. Think about what you enjoyed and what you felt some resistance around. Where there is resistance, there is space for healing. Pull out your journal today. Reflect on where your resistance is, and why you think this area of passion is giving you pause.

August 16

Passion can sometimes feel like slowing down or allowing yourself to sink into the day rather than race through it. There is something delicious about only having one or two things to move through on any given day—it creates space for deeper experiences and interactions. See where you can slow down your tasks today. Spend more time on the energy of creating solutions and connections. When you feel yourself trying to rush through a moment, pause and take a breath. Your angel wants you to truly feel your way through your day. Notice all the sensory experiences, not just the ones that seem efficient and productive. Explore your world slowly. Savor each moment as if it was a mouthful of scrumptious food to ground the energy of passion into your day and moments, giving you permission to enjoy it on a mundane yet magical level.

August 17

As we age, we start to notice a pattern of talking ourselves out of doing things we really want to do, explaining why we can't have experiences the soul really wants to have. Money and time are usually the bad guys in justifying why a desire cannot be fulfilled. The truth is that every time you do this, you disconnect a little more from the energy of passion. In turn, disconnection can foster resentment that can quickly turn to anger, the destructive side of passion. While you shouldn't always give in to your desires without question or pause, consider whether you have any that are healthy, life-affirming, and safe to explore today. If so, take action: let yourself be swept up in the joy and hope that this sort of passion brings.

August 18

Today, passion feels more like self-care and self-love. Your angels find it funny that humans think of self-care as a luxury and not a daily honor of passion. In a way, taking care of yourself is the ultimate in exploring passion; seeing yourself as a divine temple allows you to see others the same way. Today, Solis wants you to start listing all the ways you can honor and care for yourself. It might be a massage, a trip to your hair stylist, a romantic date with a partner, or even sitting in the sunshine while having lunch and watching the birds. There is no wrong or right way to bring this level of passion into your day. If you are still not sure where to start, take a slow and steady breath and just feel for a nudge from Solis. Your guardians are always full of good ideas.

August 19

Passion is an energy that can bring with it a lot of movement and has the ability to change things in your life, perhaps in ways you will love or maybe in ways you aren't very happy about. It's normal to see both sides of the coin when movement occurs, even when directing the flow of passion energy. Today you might find your passion moving you even closer to one of your dreams while also moving you further away from people who do not believe in you or support you, which is natural and how movement created by passion works. Today, keep in mind that passion can drive you toward what is in your heart and away from energy that leaks and drains your heart. Know that your passion and your heart are conspiring for your better good. Trust that your heart knows exactly what is going to bring you joy, abundance, and love.

August 20

Passion is about knowing what you truly desire, not what your ego thinks it wants. These desires burn through your whole body, like a flame that lights the way down a path you would have never considered. The energy of passion overrides logic, triggering the central nervous system and asking it to get ready for the ride of its life. People, places, and things line up in ways you would never have been able to manipulate on purpose. The energy of what you desire is potent, powerful, and has the potential to create worlds. Designed by your heart, your world becomes carved out by passion's energy. As you move through your day, notice how passion is pushing you toward what you desire. Don't think about it—move with it and observe. Be the spectator to your personal passion adventure and just watch the magic it reveals.

CHECK-IN TWO

You have now had twenty days working with your theme of passion and your angel Solis. It is time to pull out your journal and see how the prompts have been helping you stay in the energy of passion. Starting with the following prompt, make lists of tangible results or situations where your angel's assistance has aided you: "So far this month, I have _____." Once you are done, continue with the remainder of the month.

August 21

Most times, passion is about getting up and doing things you either don't want to do or have never done before. We have the tendency to only move or act when things feel good, fun, and comfortable but it's very rare for passion to work in this way. For the most part, passion will push you to do things that are new, strange, and uncomfortable. Today may very well be one of those days where your passion energy wants to push you out of the feeling of knowing and into the world of the unknown. This urge arises from the realization that everything you want and desire are not known—if they were, you would already have them. Having the urge means your heart is charting new territory, forging new paths. Your passion is moving you toward the things your heart craves. Are you as excited about today as we are?

August 22

Today is one of those days where it all comes together: you have breakthroughs big and small, the pieces seem to start falling into place, and everything you have been working toward starts to feel real and approaching the inevitable conclusion of its journey. This feeling of elation, mixed with a slight wave of exhaustion, is passion as it grounds itself in the physical world. This is the last stage of the creation process for passion, but there may still be work that needs to be done. Perhaps there's even a lot of it if you need to move physical aspects of your life around. Your angel knows it might feel like time to take a nap, but today, resist that urge. Instead, allow yourself to celebrate your breakthroughs and make a list of the last little things that need to be done today.

August 23

When we are focused on a goal, our vision tends to become very contracted. We narrow our energy and emotions to bring something into our life. Once things start to come together, we need to exhale, open ourselves up, and create space. Your passion energy is primed and ready to help create this spaciousness in your day. Bring it up from your belly into your heart with slow, gentle breaths. See it light you up, expanding your chest and pushing out the subtle bodies like a breeze does to a sail, causing movement. The more you sink into your breath today, the more space you will create within you and all around you.

August 24

We have mentioned a few times this month how passion energy can nudge you toward something that is expansive and stretchy to your skill set. Today passion is wanting to move you toward one of your secret dreams, one you hold in your heart, that you have held fear around. Today your angel and the energy of passion want to see if you can drop that fear and resistance just a little. Consider exploring this nudge from a hypothetical angle and see what happens. Who knows, you might just be surprised to find what's waiting for you on the other side of your resistance.

August 25

There will be moments in life where the rush of passion is totally unexpected and barrels into you, taking you by surprise. It might seem like a sneak attack, but your angels have been trying to get your attention for a while—they created something so big and powerful you could not ignore it. They did it this way because when an experience is meant for you, it has to come to you, regardless of how many times you miss the signs or ignore the call. Today, be mindful of when and where you find yourself being surprised, moved, or jolted into a new state of feeling—this is your angels bringing you what is yours in all of its divine beauty.

August 26

Sometimes passion is an exchange of ideas, a space where all involved can expand and learn something new. It is not a mistake that humans are all different and have individual views and perspectives about the world and their place in it. It is in the exploration of difference that new solutions are created. This is glorious. Today, be open to having a conversation—not a conflict—with others who have a different approach, a new thought, or a contrasting idea. Be willing to explore what they say without judgment, and allow space for passion energy to flow through. You do not have to agree at the end of your discussion; sometimes agreeing to disagree is a fabulous result. Even in these cases, you can still learn things. See something from a new angle and immerse yourself in the flow of passion.

August 27

Passion energy is flowing through you even when you don't know what you want and seem to be in a constant state of confusion. It is passion that pushes you to seek clarity and question all that is, was, and could be. This state of not knowing but feeling the pull to know has all been sparked by your desire for something more. The need you feel is not born out of lack but through a pull to grow beyond where you are and see what else is possible for you. This does not mean you are ungrateful for what you have and have created—it means that, like the universe in which you live, you are ready to create something new and allow the energy of passion to flow through you and into the physical world once again. Embrace this first stage of the process. The details may not be clear, but the process will bring you closer to clarity if you allow it to.

August 28

Today you will find out that passion feels a lot like trust—you will trust the nudge, path, and growth that will take place by allowing passion energy to flow into your day. It isn't easy to do new things, take unknown steps, or let new people into your life. Today, your angel is asking you to do exactly these things. Someone new may enter your life; a new opportunity may present itself; or you might have to take a new way to your job, the supermarket, or your favorite coffee shop. It might all seem random at first, but you and I both know there is no such thing as coincidence. Everything that happens today has been mapped, aligned, and organized by the vortex of energy you have created with your passion. Really, all you have to do is trust yourself, and that shouldn't be hard as long as you remember that you are an incredible creator!

August 29

As your month of passion winds down, it may help to go over all the positive things that working with passion energy has brought into your life. Identify the moments, people, or situations that happened as a direct result of following the direction your passion sent you over the last month. Make a list of all the wonderful and amazing ways passion has affected your daily life. Give thanks for each item on your list as you show gratitude for these divine blessings. It is also a good time to think about when and where you will intentionally bring more passion into your life in the future. This isn't the only month of your life focused on passion—you can continue to work with this energy for as long or as often as you so choose. As you have seen this month, sometimes bringing more passion into your life can be a very good thing.

August 30

As you finish your month working with your angel of passion, think about all the areas in which you felt resistance and/or doubt related to how and when passion showed up. It is completely normal to feel these emotions, especially when presented with new ideas, situations, or people. The more clarity you can have around your points of resistance, the better you can forge a path forward. Remember to be kind and compassionate with yourself, and do your best not to judge when you didn't respond to the nudges passion sent your way. It is normal to hesitate and seek more information before acting. Everything you have done this month has given you space to grow and explore, and that's all the angels ever wanted for you.

Closing Ceremony for the Month

Your time with angel Solis has now come to an end, for this year anyway. It is time to pack up your altar for the angel of passion. You might want to keep the items you have gathered this month as a reminder of how passion energy opened new doors, created new opportunities, or even brought you new interests. Perhaps some of these new things you will continue with even though your time with Solis is complete for now. It is important to give your altar and other spaces you may have used during your time with angel Solis a good cleaning as a way of closing the energy that you have been working with over the past month. Wash your magical items, wipe down your altar's surface, and put any cards or images away. Remember to wave a smoking herb bundle over the space, so that you can cleanse and reset the energy, preparing it for the next angel. As you clean and reset your altar, say a small prayer of thanks:

Angel Solis, I thank thee
For showing me how to be
A light
A spark
A beacon of passion
For giving me faith
Showing me the path of trust
And bringing new experiences to me
We played
We danced
We binge-watched TV
I am thankful for your time with me
For now, I clean and clear this sacred workspace
This altar I cleanse
To honor you
To honor the work we have done.
Thank you.

Chapter Ten
SEPTEMBER

Sylvania
The Angel of Transitions

Welcome to September, the month of transitions. In this chapter, you will learn about an area of your day that you have probably never even thought about. I know transitions were not something I personally gave a lot of thought to until the angels started teaching me about them. Now I am wondering how I even made it without understanding the importance of these spaces, gaps, and connection points in my day. It is Sylvania's hope that after you have worked through this chapter, you too will see how essential these parts of your day are. Throughout this month your angel will offer lessons, messages, and guidance around transitions that could take the form of instructional tasks to ground the lesson. The meditations, observations, and guidance itself may sometimes be more abstract, as it is channeled material. Just know that whatever you personally receive from the daily prompt is correct and valid. Transitions do not just affect your day—they are natural and occur all around us, monthly, yearly, and hourly. This chapter may be one of the most important ones you will read because it could change the way you think about your day—it certainly did for me.

Connection Prayer: Bringing in the Energy of the Angel of Transitions

To get the most out of your month with the angel Sylvania, set up your September altar. You can include your favorite angel card or tarot cards. I highly recommend cards like the Empress, the Seven of Pentacles, Five of Cups, Six of Swords, and the Wheel of Fortune, as these cards represent various forms of transition and change. I also suggest leaving space on your altar to add things to it as you move through your month. Once you have your altar cleansed and set up, light your candle. This month I recommend using white candles, as they represent the energy of everything yet nothing, like a pause in your energy. When you are ready to light your candle, say the following prayer to bring in the energy of angel Sylvania and connect them to your September:

Angel Sylvania, I summon thee;
To help find
The gaps in between
The spaces I have been ignoring
The energy leaks in my day
Show me how to plug them
Raise my awareness
Teach me some tricks
On how to leverage this energy
With your help
Life will begin to flow
And my energy
It will glow
Transitions will be my superpower
With you by my side
I bind you to my September calendar
Together for this month-long ride
I am ready to start
Let us not delay
With these words now done
Let's start today!

Messages for the Days of the Month
September 1

For the most part, you may not notice transitions in your day. From waking to falling back to sleep, you will pass through many different activities throughout your day. Each one will have a transition point; the space between is an opportunity for magic and miracles. This month, your angel Sylvania wants to bring your focus to these moments of your day and show you how to use them to create space, calm, and grounded energy so you can always feel energized and alive. Learning about these transition moments is important, as you can use a lot of energy if you don't stop and honor them. Not knowing how to use transitions can contribute to increased stress, fatigue, and mental exhaustion. Today, when you go to bed, recap all the things that happened during your day, highs and lows. Then wrap them in a pink bubble and send them away to your angel. This visualization helps you let go of the day and moves you into rest. Well done—transition one is complete!

September 2

Can you think of two tasks that you normally move from one to the other without thinking about? Perhaps it is from social media to emails, emails to dealing with clients, or driving home and then launching into domestic diva mode. Today, your angel asks that you identify two tasks in your daily life and hold sixty seconds of transition space between them. It can be as simple as stopping when you pull your car into your driveway, placing your hand on your heart, and breathing deeply while gently disconnecting from everything that happened before that moment, giving it to the angels. Once those sixty seconds are up, move into your divine domestic self. If you are pausing between email and social media, do the same. Whatever task you normally rush into, place one brief gap in your day and invite your angel in.

September 3

It is not only your day that is filled with transitions—your year has four major transitions woven into its fabric. You call them the seasons, and the angels like to call them soul transitions. Each moves you into a different energy of the soul. No matter where you live on the planet, you will be having a season right now, a transition from one energy to the next. Summer to autumn is a move from long days with lots of activities to shorter days and calmer energy. Winter to spring brings you out of a period of reflection and into one of growth. As you move through these transitions, you will notice your soul seeks different things. It searches for specific people, opportunities, and situations to enhance the transition that is taking place. Today, take a moment to think about what you are seeking right now and consider how it is being driven by the season you now find yourself in. What you find may just surprise you.

September 4

When you start becoming more aware of how transitions show up in your day, you start to realize they are everywhere, even when you eat. There are gaps, spaces in between each mouthful of food. These gaps allow you to bring in gratitude for the food you are eating. When you put your utensils down between bites and chew slowly, you create a way to move intentionally through the process of eating. This intention honors the nourishment the food gives your body, and helps you see meals as more than just one more thing you need to strike off your to-do list. Allow each bite and spoonful to be an experience all its own, and thank the food for fueling, healing, and serving your body. You will see how small transitions can make even a simple meal a devotional practice.

September 5

Transitions always occur after something has ended. The transition could be large, like leaving a job or ending a relationship, or it could be small, like finishing the next thing on your to-do list or moving from one domestic task to another. Either way, an ending has unfolded. Today you are being asked by your angel to honor the endings that have led to your transitions and see them as something sacred, no matter their size. When you get into the cycle of honoring the cause of transition, you no longer fear endings. Instead, you begin to see them as the natural step in a cycle, process, or journey. The more you can move through these endings with grace, the more potent your transitions will become. Your angel asks you to examine the endings in your life and give them space—especially the ones happening today. Acknowledge them, thank them, and then let them slip away so you can move on.

September 6

Transitions happen just before something new begins. They are exciting moments in which you realize you are about to start or create something, have a new or different conversation, or engage in an experience you have yet to have today. In this respect, transitions are filled with possibilities and opportunities, which is another reason they are so very important to the flow of your day. If managed correctly, transitions can and do set the tone of the experience yet to come, paving the way for how things will unfold and how you will feel about the next step. Today your angel is asking you to use these transition moments in your day to pump yourself up. Be your own cheerleader! Get yourself excited and flood your body with energetic vibes—it will do two amazing things to your mind and body: it will drop your attention firmly into the present moment (which it loves to be in), and it will get your focus out of your head. Only miracles are possible in this state, and it all happens in your transitions.

September 7

Stop. Take a breath—a proper one. Inhale deeply through your nose and exhale with a sigh through your mouth. Do it again. One more time, in and out. Now, gently just bounce on your feet. Now do ten bounces. Unclench your jaw. And now take a last breath. Well done. That was a beautiful transition. You moved ever so gently from one moment into the next. You stopped, connected, and got energy moving throughout your entire body. It was so simple, yet super powerful. Repeat this exercise as many times as you feel necessary today and see how you feel by the time you crawl into bed. Maybe you will find yourself nice and calm or a little less drained. No matter how you feel, you will have given yourself valuable chances to breathe with intention; your body, mind, and soul will celebrate it.

September 8

Not all transitions are small. There are very large transitions that happen over the course of a human life: at the end of a relationship, when a loved one passes away, leaving home, starting a family, changing careers, and at retirement. There is a good chance you or someone you know is in a longer transition period right now. Unlike the smaller ones you experience every day, these longer ones ask you to hold more space and require you to lean into them and surrender to their energy. These transitions might even require you to pause and be still. Most importantly, longer transitions ask you not to judge. Today, your angel wants you to practice compassion when dealing with these types of transitions: compassion for yourself if you are traversing them, and compassion for another if they are amid this change. Open your heart and let it guide you.

September 9

For the most part, transitions happen when we aren't paying attention. The problem is that when we aren't mindful of the gaps, pauses, and spaces in between, we tend to create energy leaks. Energy leaks happen when energy keeps draining away because we have not stopped to close it, reset it, and restart it with a new task or intention. This sort of leak brings with it fatigue, brain fog, a lack of focus, and can cause restlessness and irritation. It is not your fault when this happens to you. We aren't generally taught about transitions; most of us grew up in a culture that tells us to "carry on" without time to stop—we must keep moving. This attitude leads to feeling overwhelmed, increases in stress and anxiety, and a workforce that is so exhausted it would rather resign than continue. Luckily for you, you have a guardian angel looking over you. Now you know how to increase your energy, stop your leaks, and use the potent power of transitions in your daily life.

September 10

Today, your angel wants you to be on the lookout for places you may be stuck in a transition. It is very easy to stay in a space that appears to have no demands or doesn't ask you to make any important or life-changing decisions. Often, the ego will lull us into a sense of paralysis so we won't do anything stupid, like change our lives and go for our dreams. The mind creates a space: you now know it's called a transition, and it makes you believe that is the safest place in the world to be. You will know right away when you are stuck mid-transition: you will feel as though there's no point to anything, and crushing feelings of apathy and pointlessness will overwhelm you. You will probably even hear yourself say things such as "I'm just going through the motions," all of which is a sign that you are well and truly stuck in a transition. The good news is that you now know about it, so you can get yourself unstuck by doing something totally wild and crazy (okay, or just something different).

CHECK-IN ONE

It has now been ten days since you started working with the angel Sylvania and the theme of transitions. Now is the ideal time to visit your altar and consider if the items you set it up with are still relevant or if you need to switch them out or add to them. It is also time to give your altar space a bit of a clean, freshen up any cut flowers, and light your candles once more. Say a small prayer or mantra, or sit in silent meditation for a couple of minutes. This small journey to your altar will bring your mind, body, and soul back to a place of devotion and recenter you in the theme of the month.

September 11

There is something wonderful about being in a space where nobody wants anything from you, where you are safe, secure, and allowed to just drop your shoulders and unclench your jaw for a bit. There is a sense of ease in this sort of space, where everything else drops away and leaves you feeling more like yourself and less like the projection or persona you choose for social situations. The power of transition is in its gift of breathing room, small pockets of stillness, and the pauses that allow you to remember who you are and why you are making the decisions you are. When we give ourselves moments throughout the day to drop back into this place, we can make sure we are moving through our day with intention, not reaction. Stop for a moment and drop into a pause. Think about all that you have done today and all that is left to do. Make sure you are doing it for the correct reasons. Breathe. And then carry on.

September 12

When a powerful emotion arises during your day, it can push you into a transition. You could be doing something one moment and then suddenly you are overtaken and your mind's focus has wandered from what you are doing and instead is hooked on the memory attached to that arising emotion. These transitions are incredibly distracting and can often throw off your mood and derail your day. Yet so few people understand these as transition moments. Today, if a powerful emotion sideswipes you, your angel wants you to follow your transition protocols: Stop. Acknowledge the shift. Breathe. Release. Carry on with what you were doing before the emotion swept in. If the emotion is particularly powerful, you might want to do the bouncing exercise the guardians introduced you to. If you still need to bring yourself back to your body and ground into the moment, tap your collarbone gently as you bounce. The better you understand the temporary nature of these moments, the less power they will have over you.

September 13

Today, look for fun and playful interruptions. These are the universe's way of bringing more joy into your life through the act of transition. Gaps, breaks, and points of interruption are all transition points. There is no law written anywhere in the universe that says they can't also be fun, playful, and filled with belly laughs. Be on the lookout for the small moments that make you giggle, flashes that make you smile, and gaps that are filled with pure joy. Your world is a magical place, and you get to drop into that magic whenever you want. Think of these interruptions as magical portals that are ready to move you from one reality to another, laughing all the way.

September 14

Not everything in your day will go according to plan. Time may slip by faster than you anticipated. You might end up with an important task that wasn't on your already crazy to-do list. Or perhaps uninvited guests arrive at your house just when you thought you were going to have time to watch some TV. It is in these moments that knowing how transitions work that will save you. Being able to just stop, breathe, and regroup will make you more resilient and won't allow these impromptu moments to throw you off-balance. When you are equipped with connection points, tools that bring you back to the moment, it is hard for the outside world to break your stride.

September 15

Sometimes a transition is a strategic interruption, a gap you create so that you will stop a behavior or break a habit that is not healthy, constructive, or productive. This could be a space in which you shift after you find yourself worrying about the future. It could also be the grounding point you align yourself to when you feel your thoughts rambling. It can also be intentional to bring you back on task so you can get back in the flow with your work day. Transitions do happen as a result of something naturally ending, but they can also be created to interrupt patterns that do not serve you. Today, your angel wants you to use your transitions in an affirming way to move you from a space you do not wish to be in to one you do. When using transitions this way, they become pattern disruptors and intention creators that have the power to change the course of your day.

September 16

Transitions are very much like when the Moon goes void of course, an astrological phrase that describes the period after the Moon has made an aspect with one zodiac sign but has yet to enter the next one. The space between zodiac signs simply exists without any need to impress or influence. This is a lovely place to be in, one that allows you to decide what your experience of it will be like: Is it rest? A place of ease? A place of gentle flow? Today, your angel wants you to practice being in the void-of-course Moon's energy. Check to see when the Moon will go void of course, or create a space on your calendar for a void-of-course Moon day. See how this period of transition affects you mentally and emotionally. When the Moon is void of course describes your transitional moments; what better way to dive deep into them than by working with this energy in a more expansive and cosmic way?

September 17

When something is contained in a cage, do you think it is the bars that keep the beast inside or is the space between the bars? There is something very powerful about the illusion of space—the distance between two points and the way we judge if it is too small or too big for the action we are contemplating. There tends to be a lot of meaning shoved into the gap, stuffing it to overfull with uncertainty. Yet the space itself is nothing, air completely devoid of anything solid. Matter can pass through space swiftly and without hesitation. The mind does not like gaps; it seeks to fill them and make them into tangible things. Transitions are not solid—they hold nothing and everything at the same time. Your mind will constantly want to fill spaces like this, block them, and/or make you believe that you never have a moment to think, breathe, or pause, but this is a trick of the mind. Today, do not fall for it.

September 18

There is a moment before a plan comes together, a freeze of time as all the pieces of the manifestation hang together before snapping into place. In these moments, you realize you have been holding your breath, afraid to knock things out of alignment. At these transition points, your angel would like to remind you to breathe, release, and know that whatever has been created is now inevitable. There is nothing you can do to stop what is forming. The momentum is too strong and the energy is far too aligned for anything to stop it now. So drop your shoulders, unclench your jaw, and sink into this space, this gap, this transition. Allow yourself to honor this moment as the best use of your mental and emotional energy. Stop. Breathe. Ground. That's it.

September 19

There is a brief moment single day just before the sun breaks the horizon line, where you can start to see what is on its way, yet the world around you feels still and quiet. Once the sun comes up each day, the world changes almost instantly: birds start moving about and singing, more traffic hits the roads, and even things start to stir inside your home until the normal noise of the day is upon you. In the pause before something new begins, your angel would like you to experience one of these natural moments this week. Today your angel wants you to grab a nice warm beverage or a glass of water, find somewhere safe and comfortable to sit, and allow yourself to become one with Mother Nature's morning transition. Feel the energy of it as it moves through you and the world around you. Become one with the experiential moment that is a transition.

September 20

There is a moment when finishing up one task in which the next task begins to invade your thoughts and distract you from ending your current task. The invasive thought does its best to pull you away and move you into a continual state of cerebral drain. When this happens, just stop. Take a breath and shift your mind back to ending your current task. This transition moment will feel a lot like grounding, because that is exactly what it is. In order to maintain mental and emotional energy during the day, you need to finish your tasks completely and have a gap between starting new ones. Distractions are energy leaks that will drain you and often cause mid-afternoon slumps. Today, be mindful of where your mind is trying to pull you off-task. Practice your transition protocols and get back to finishing what you started. Not only will refocusing help with your overall energy, it will also greatly improve your mood.

CHECK-IN TWO

You have now had twenty days working with the energy of transitions and your angel Sylvania. It is time to pull out your journal and see how the prompts have been helping you stay in the flow of transitions. Starting with the following prompt, make lists of tangible results or situations where your angel's assistance has aided you: "So far this month, I have _____." Once you are done, move on to the remainder of the month.

September 21

If you have ever had to deal with paperwork or acquire official government documentation like a driver's license or a passport, you know what it means to queue up: standing in line and waiting to be called while you hold your magic number. The entire process is a lengthy transition between showing up and getting a result. The angels know that these sorts of transitions can teach you a lot about yourself. They can show you how well-prepared you are—how patient are you and how well do you do in situations where you literally have no control? In this respect these lengthy transitions become meditative learning exercises for the ego. The next time you find yourself in one, ask yourself: which part of my ego do I need to give a little love to at this moment?

September 22

There are times in life where it is better to pause than react. Take a moment before you engage your mouth. This space you create between responses is a transition. For the most part, humans respond from a reactive place and don't allow space to open up to dispel the emotional charge of a situation. But when you start to use transitions in this way, the way you engage with others will shift too. Today your angel is asking you to practice not reacting or responding to people, places, and situations right away. Practice transition protocols first: stop, breathe, bounce on your toes, and ground, and *then* see if your words and actions feel different. It won't be easy to remember to pause, initially, so be patient and kind with yourself and celebrate when you do remember. Learning this one simple transition could very well mean the difference between allowing yourself to receive more good or pushing it away.

September 23

There will be moments during the day where your mind just floats away. You will feel yourself drift off and become somewhat spacey. This is a transition, and more to the point, a forced transition. These happen when the mind needs a break between tasks but space has not yet been created for it. We all tap out mentally at some point and have moments when our brains really need a time-out—which means when you notice your mind floating away today, get up. If possible, go outside; if not, just move away from your work area and move your body. Tap your collarbone gently, tap just above the belly button gently, and bounce on your feet slowly. This gentle tapping plugs you back into your physical body and brings your focus back to the present moment. Now, take a few deep, slow breaths and move back to the task at hand.

September 24

There are moments where it is important for us to step out of our lives for a moment, by which the angels mean to go on vacation, spend a night alone, or somehow create some separation between ourselves and our daily life. This time is a self-initiated transition, a space deliberately created that allows us to stop for a moment, take a breath, gather our energy, and be still. It is so common in the world we all live in to rush from one thing to the next and not really think about how we are acting or why. Rushing drains our energy and doesn't allow for making clear decisions. Taking this sort of transition can reorient you in your life and shift you into a present and focused sense of awareness. Acting with deliberation will bring clarity and purpose to your decisions and allow you room to organize your thoughts and feelings. That sounds like a win for you, a win for your life, and a win for those who live with you.

September 25

Sometimes a transition is simply closing a door, be it physical or metaphorical. This act of closure can create a much-needed gap in your life, energy, and mood. Not all doors need to be open all the time; there will be moments where closing them is more beneficial to you. Your angel wants you to know that there is a big difference between locking a door and closing one. When a door is locked and sealed shut, anything that was flowing through that doorway is cut off. But closing a door is temporary and provides space for rest, rejuvenation, taking a breath, or pulling back your energy. If you need to, close a door today to create a transition point in your physical space. You will know when it is time to open it again and let things flow.

September 26

Today your angel would like you to create your very own transition protocol. You have learned a lot over the course of this month about where, how, and when transitions show up in your day and life. You have learned a few techniques to help you move in, out, and through each transition point, which means you have enough information on what works best for you and maybe what didn't give you the space or peace you really needed during a transition moment. Remember that your protocol can be as long or as short as you feel you need. Another thing about having spent the last three weeks learning differing transition lengths is that you will know how much time you need between tasks, projects, cycles, and events. Your angel recommends starting small and then moving on to crafting larger transition moments. Just remember to have fun—this is your time, your space, and your point of rest, release, and restoration.

September 27

Today we shift our focus to transitions in health. For the most part so far, your angel has approached transitions in very general terms. Here, though, it is time to focus and be deliberate about creating a transition that will assist your health or even complement healing work you may be undertaking. Today your angel wants you to find places in your day where it seems logical to create a transition point for the sole purpose of your health and well-being. It could be before you eat. It could be before you end your work day. It could even be between an old habit you are wanting to get rid of and a new habit you want to create. Trust that you will know exactly where this transition needs to take place, and create it.

September 28

There are moments in our lives that require a deliberate emotional transition point. They are extremely helpful when having a stressful or disruptive day, when it feels as though you can't quite get your feet under you and are instead swept up in a flow that is not positive or enjoyable. Creating intentional transition points in your day to break this sort of energy up will help you feel more in control, more emotionally stable, and less scattered. These transition points will ground you, bring you back to the moment, and allow you to create the space you need to breathe. In turn, you won't feel overwhelmed as easily. As you move through your day, be on the lookout for situations or even habits that have been making you feel anxious or uncomfortable. Create a transition moment when these feelings arise and see if the energy, direction, and flow of your emotional charge has changed. Your angel thinks you will be pleasantly surprised.

September 29

When it comes to money, creating abundance, or even attracting and maintaining wealth, you will find transitions can be extremely helpful. There are three very important parts when it comes to the manifestation process. The first part everyone does pretty well, attracting things about which they have the strongest emotional charge. The second part fewer do as well, which is holding on to what one has attracted. The third part is the most difficult: growing and nurturing what has been attracted so it can be leveraged for further manifestation. Today your angel wants you to think about where you can create transitions to assist you with parts two and three of the manifestation process. Really consider how you could hold on to something without slipping into old spending patterns. Think about how you can create spaces for your money to grow and how you will hold energy to nourish and support your money over the long term. It might be as simple as taking that jar of coins and putting it in a savings or investment account, rather than the cash machine and spending it right away.

September 30

Over this month you have learned a lot about the why and how of transitions. Your angel would like you to leave this month thinking about all the transitions in your life as part of your larger spiritual practice. See the art of creating and honoring gaps and in-between spaces as a devotional practice in which your subtle and vibrational bodies have a moment to come together and align as one. Make space in your daily life that allows you to plug in and connect with all the parts of who you are. It can be so easy to forget you are whole and divinely supported throughout your day, so let this simple practice help you stop and tune in to the support, guidance, and wisdom from your higher self and of course your angels that is always with you. As you practice your transitions today, listen. See if you can hear the whispers of that guidance and trust that it always has your back.

Closing Ceremony for the Month

Your time with angel Sylvania has now come to an end, for this year anyway. It is time to pack up your altar for the angel of transitions. It is important to give your altar and other spaces you may have used a good cleaning as a way of closing the energy that you have been working with over the past month. Wash your magical items, wipe down your altar surface, and put any cards or images away. Remember, also, to wave a smoking herb bundle over the space so that you can cleanse the energy and prepare it for the next angel. As you clean and reset your altar, say a small prayer of thanks:

> *Angel Sylvania, I thank thee*
> *For showing me how to just be*
> *Together we created space*
> *Took a breath*

Found the gaps
Seeded magic
My day is more intentional
My energy feels more in-flow
I know our time together
Has helped me grow
Transitions are my new superpower
I am so grateful for this time
For now, I clean and clear this sacred workspace
This altar I cleanse
To honor you
To honor the work we have done.
Thank you.

Chapter Eleven
OCTOBER

Chana
The Angel of Gratitude

Welcome to October, the month of gratitude. I know what you are thinking—"More gratitude?" I get it, it feels overdone. It's like everywhere you look, someone is telling you to be more grateful. The angels and I totally understand that this area of teaching feels like it has been taught to death. But here is the thing: it works. And there are so many different ways to bring the energy of gratitude into your daily life. Throughout this month, your angel is going to give you lessons, messages, and guidance around gratitude that could take the form of instructional tasks, which will ground the lesson. The meditations, observations, and sometimes the guidance itself may be more abstract, as it is channeled material. Just know that whatever you personally receive from the daily prompt is correct and valid. I know that the angels have helped me see so many different ways to play with this energy, and your angel of the month, Chana, is hoping you will give her the opportunity to show you as well. I am especially excited for you to learn the art of thanking things forward.

Connection Prayer: Bringing in the Energy of the Angel of Gratitude

To get the most out of your month with the angel Chana, set up your October altar. It would be wonderful to create a vision board of all the things you have been grateful for this year so far. Keep your board relevant to the current year, as we are building a vortex of energy based on a twelve-month cycle. I also suggest leaving space on your altar to add things to it as you move through your month, such as another vision board for all the things you want to manifest. Once you have your altar cleansed and set up, light your candle. This month, I recommend using pink candles (representing the energy of the heart) or green or gold (representing abundance). On the vibrational level, gratitude and abundance work hand in hand. Of course if you cannot find any of these candles, just simple white tea lights will be fine. When you are ready to light your candle, say the following prayer to bring in the energy of angel Chana and connect them to your October:

> *Angel Chana, I summon thee;*
> *Breathe life into gratitude for me*
> *Show me how to thank again*
> *Allow me to find magic within*
> *Point to my abundant good*
> *Where miracles live*
> *And magic recedes*
> *I am open and willing to receive*
> *All the gratitude that I need*
> *I bind you now to my October*
> *As these words are said and done*
> *This journey has now begun.*

Messages for the Days of the Month
October 1

Gratitude is not new—it's a topic that has been covered for a while now, and Chana wants you to understand that there is a really good reason for it: gratitude can change beliefs, alter emotions, and even manifest dreams. There are many different ways to bring gratitude into your life; one of the simplest is to say the words "thank you" more often. These two words can become a blessing in your day and send massive ripples of positive energy outward from you and toward all those who come in contact with you. Two little words, so much power. Thank your body when you wake up. Thank your clothes when you dress. Thank your food when you eat. Thank your car/bus/train when you need to travel. Thank angel Chana at the end of the day for providing you with so many things to be thankful for. What an incredible day you are about to have!

October 2

When we step fully into the portal of gratitude, everything has the potential to change. The way we feel about life can change; the way we engage with things can change, and relationships might even begin to change—especially the relationship you have with yourself. Today your angel wants you to find at least three things about yourself that you are grateful for. Perhaps it is your organizational skills, your laundry moves, or maybe just how well you treat yourself. Although there will be time to count your blessings in the external world, today you are being asked to keep your focus solely on yourself. When you can be grateful for who you are, the life you are getting to create, and the inspired divine energy that pumps through you, everyone around you can, too. Three things, that's it—go be grateful for you.

October 3

Your body works hard and does so many things without you even knowing about it. It supports you, moves you, allows you to engage and participate in the world of the senses, heals you, and never ever judges you. The flesh and bone vessel that carries your soul from incarnation to incarnation is a miraculous thing indeed. So today, angel Chana wants you to be in ceremony with your body. Find as many things as possible to be grateful for when it comes to your physical expression. It is time to work together with your body and allow it to feel loved, honored, and acknowledged. You would not be reading this without your eyes, so thank them. You would not be breathing without your lungs, so thank them. You would not be able to enjoy walking without your feet and legs, so thank them. We all take so many of the things the body does for granted, so let's shift out of that way of thinking and instead go to a place of devotional gratitude for all the body temple does for you.

October 4

Gratitude can often feel like a form of surrender—you stop focusing on what you don't have and instead move fully into embracing what is right in front of you. It is so easy to let the ego dictate the terms of your experience through lack and comparison. It can invade your thoughts and manipulate your emotions, making you feel less-than or behind somehow. But here in the portal of gratitude, you get to sink into the magic of everything you have personally created that your divine energy has brought forth, and everything that was manifested by you and for you. Your angels would like you to make a list of all the amazing things you have personally created or manifested. See if you can get this list up to thirty items and then bless each of them by simply saying thank you.

October 5

Gratitude can feel a lot like saying yes: to what you have, to what you are creating, to what you let go of, and to everything spinning in the co-creation energy of the Divine. Every day, you are presented with opportunities to say yes. It could be to something new coming into your life or letting a part of your life know you are happy to be engaging and experiencing it. Today, look for places where you get to say yes—this is where your gratitude lives. Creating a vortex of yeses will allow the universe to bring you even more things to say yes to. Of course, you don't have to say yes to everything that crosses your path, but if your heart—and not your head—booms with the word *yes*, then speak it. Let your soul recognize itself in a joyous moment co-created with your angels to bring you something you desire. That's truly something to be grateful for.

October 6

Sometimes gratitude can feel like a prayer or a way of communing with something more powerful than your human self. Your angel knows that prayer is a way of speaking the energy of thanks into the world. It can be about rejoicing in the gifts one has been bestowed. To clarify, we are not talking about the type of prayer done in a church—we are talking about everyday prayer, the small conversations you have with that which you call the Divine. This dialogue comes from your heart. It is pure in its joy, passion, and even excitement. It is the direct emotional expression of your gratitude—which is the most powerful prayer you can speak. As you move through your day, think about offering a few more prayers of thanks as you move through your to-do list. You don't have to do many, just two or three scattered throughout your day. See how the energy of the day unfolds. We believe it will amaze you.

October 7

Oftentimes when people think about gratitude, it amounts to lists of things they are thankful for, which is fantastic, and your angel encourages you to do this as often as possible. Yet it can also be very powerful to find one thing in your day and focus your gratitude on it. For you see, the longer you can hold something or someone in the energy of gratitude, the more you amplify that feeling. So today your task is to find one thing or one person that you are grateful for. Place your hand on your heart and list a couple of reasons why you are so grateful for this person or thing. Continue this practice throughout the day, keeping the focus on the one thing or person only. Dive deeper and deeper into why you are so grateful. It is easy to write random lists of stuff you are grateful for, but it is truly magical when you can make a list of why you are grateful for one thing or one person only.

October 8

Today, let's talk about being grateful for your life—not the one you think you should be living or the one you have lived, but the fact that right here, in this moment, you are alive. It is a miracle. Life is a gift and not to be taken for granted. It is easy to forget life is fleeting and temporary as you walk around and deal with your day-to-day life. Time moves quickly, and each moment is something to be grateful for. It is easy to take your life for granted, to presume you will wake up again tomorrow and press "repeat" on your existence. This is not the case, however. Just for today, celebrate being alive. Rejoice in being able to take a breath. Raise a glass to being able to speak to people you love. And find a way to elevate the energy of hope around your daily tasks. You are a magical miraculous creation, and you have made it to another day.

October 9

Today, your gratitude angel wants you to focus on one person you are truly grateful to have in your life. This person does not have to be physically present in your life; it could be someone who has crossed over, as long as you are grateful for how they molded and shaped your current experience. This person could also be your boss, coach, spiritual advisor, partner, or even someone you met briefly who dramatically changed your life for the better. Once you have your person in mind, write a list of ten reasons why you are so grateful for this person with details on how and why you are so grateful about these things. The more detail you can write, the deeper the vortex of gratitude becomes. This also seeds your gratitude vortex to bring you more people like the one you are celebrating today. Open your heart, pick up your pen, and write your thanks to just the one person who has moved you in a way no other has.

October 10

Have you ever spent time being grateful for something you do not have? This is a process called "thanking it forward," and it is a powerful manifestation method that today, your angel Chana wants you to practice. This form of gratitude is not meant to amplify the feelings of lack in your life. So if you feel yourself drifting into focusing on what you don't have, stop for a minute. Gently tap your collarbone a couple times, take a few deep breaths, and drop into the present moment once again. All you have to do is think about a thing or experience in your heart that you would really like to have and thank it for existing and showing up in your life. Be so grateful that this is available to you, and thank the feeling that having this thing or experience will bring you. Really sink into the feelings it will bring you and let a wave of gratitude wash over you. Imagine, breathe, tap, thank. Simple. You might even create a vision board for this and add it to your October altar.

CHECK-IN ONE

It has now been ten days since you started working with the angel Chana and the theme of gratitude. Now is the ideal time to visit your altar and consider if the items you set it up with are still relevant or if you need to switch them out or add to them. It is also time to give your altar space a bit of a clean, freshen up any cut flowers, and light your candles once more. Say a small prayer or mantra, or sit in silent meditation for a couple of minutes. This small journey to your altar will bring your mind, body, and soul back to a place of devotion and center you in the theme of the month.

October 11

It is not very often people take a moment to bless all the things in their lives that stay exactly the same. Humans are by nature expansive beings, always wanting to create something new and fresh. Yet it is easy to forget that the main reason we feel creative energy is because of all the things in life that stay the same. The constant, stable energy this level of sameness brings you is the very key to your manifestation powers. It might be the smallest of things, like your energy bill always being the same amount every single month. Maybe it's your morning cup of coffee or tea or your special chair. These are things to be grateful for; they hold more power than you could possibly imagine. Today, your angel would like you to be grateful for all that is constant in your life, everything that shows up identically again and again. These things are portals through which miracles can occur. Thank them, bless them, and never take them for granted.

October 12

Today you are being asked by your angel to be grateful for the unexpected. Most humans aren't overly keen on surprises; I happen to be one of them (they freak me out). But the angels have taught me that not all surprises or unexpected events need to be horrible. In fact, if we get into the habit of blessings and being grateful for happy surprises, we set up a vortex of energy that allows us to experience more joyful moments, which is why you are being guided to open a space of gratitude for the unexpected. Rejoice in the unknown as it crosses your path and set a vibration of gleeful anticipation for the gifts that are on their way to you. It isn't always easy to feel this way, especially when many of us grew up in families where the element of surprise had the potential to lead to horrible outcomes. But that expectation is a learned response, and anything we learn can be unlearned and replaced. Today is the day you begin the relearning process, and you are going to do it with the energy of gratitude and the help of the angels.

October 13

Today, your angel is asking you to see how you show gratitude to your guides, the Divine, and all the other members of your spiritual team. Do you acknowledge their part when things actually go as you asked? Do you stop and say thank you when things line up just as you prayed they would? Giving an offering or honoring the help and assistance you constantly receive from the vibrational world is a deeply profound act of gratitude. It is easy to take for granted all the things that seem to effortlessly happen in your life, just as it is easy to remember the times when you were on your knees begging for divine intervention. Sometimes the gap between the petition and the result is vast, other times it is not. Starting today, make a commitment to include your spirit team in your gratitude work. Everyone likes to be thanked for a job well done and your spirit team is no different.

October 14

Sometimes the best form of gratitude is saying nothing at all and just listening. Your gratitude angel knows the feeling of living in a world where everyone wants to be heard but very few people want to stop and listen. Today your angel is asking you to be the person who is listening. Honor another person by putting your phone down, looking them in the eye, and really connecting to them. This form of space-holding is a sacred act and one that means more to people than words ever really could. How wonderful will it feel to be able to give someone you care about this gift today, to form a connection that isn't just transactional but intentional? There really isn't a better way to thank someone for being a part of your life.

October 15

You have been practicing gratitude in multiple forms for a couple of weeks now, from listing, to saying thank you to things you have yet to manifest, and listening. Today is a very good day to reflect on how these practices might have changed you. Grab your journal and a pen, and look for clues or signs of how staying in the energy of gratitude has changed your daily life. Is it just that your thoughts are more positive? Have people been treating you differently? Make note of whatever seems to have shifted while you have been going through this month's journey with your angel. If you can't think of anything, that is also fine, but make a note of it. This exercise is not a test; there are no wrong or right answers. This task of observation helps you explore and document if anything has changed in the way you interact with the world around you. Once you have finished writing, say thank you and carry on with your day.

October 16

There are moments in a day where something will activate a memory of where you used to be, people you used to hang out with, and places you used to live. This moment will allow you to reflect on how far you have come in the journey that is your life and bring a smile to your face and a warm glow to your heart. This is a feeling of gratitude, a wave of thanks for making decisions that created a future that makes you feel safe, secure, and joyful. When one of those moments washes over you today, close your eyes, place your hand on your heart, and breathe into it. Let the feeling pulse all the way through your body and leave with your exhale. This simple act will ground that gratitude in your body, allowing it to move with you throughout the rest of your day.

October 17

Although it is tempting to focus only on the big, loud, and proud things in your life, your angel wants you to look for small, seemingly insignificant things to be grateful for today. Things like a pen, or a fork, or a "good morning" from your partner are little parts of your day where the real miracles happen. Magic resides in the things we take for granted, so today, think small to create something big. Acknowledge all the small bits and pieces that make the larger canvas of your life and thank them. A painting is many small strokes, much like your life. Find the strokes, thank them, and see how the energy of the entire picture shifts and changes.

October 18

Today your angel of gratitude wants you to be thankful for time—more specifically, delayed time, or time that won't seem to hurry up. These are the places and spaces in your life where you think things are dragging on and you just want them to hurry up. What you see as a delay is actually the universe arranging things so they can fall into place easily and effortlessly. The more you try to push things, the more difficult your experience may become. Instead, sink into deep gratitude for a caring universe that is more than happy to accommodate your need for gentle, perfect, intentional alignment. The fact that the only crinkle in your day is impatience just proves that the universe is doing its job correctly.

October 19

When you think about everything you have learned over the course of your life, what is the one lesson you are most grateful for? Today your angel is asking you to thank, bless, and revel in one of your greatest lessons. See it as the beacon of expansion it was, and honor it with your praise and admiration. Regardless of whether the lesson was easy or hard and difficult, it has played a part in shaping who you are in this moment and altered how you think or possibly influenced how you feel. More than likely, the lesson taught you how to engage with the world. This lesson is a gift that keeps on giving. Today, a situation may arise that this lesson prepared you for. What an incredible thing to be grateful for.

October 20

Your angel wants you to acknowledge that you are at the receiving end of a process or cycle, and this is indeed a time to open your arms wide, expand your heart with each breath, and sing your gratitude out loud. Just make sure most of that gratitude is aimed at yourself. Without your ability to move through all the steps and do all the work, none of this would have been possible. Well done, you are amazing. You gratitude angel would like you to write yourself a thank-you letter. Acknowledge all the things you've had to overcome, work through, and heal to be here in this moment right here, right now. Fill the letter with as much emotion as you can. This letter is just for you; no one else ever has to see it. So dig deep, open your heart to yourself, and say thank you.

CHECK-IN TWO

You have now had twenty days working with your theme of gratitude and your angel Chana. It is time to pull out your journal and
see how the prompts have been helping you stay in the energy of
gratitude. Starting with the following prompt, make lists of tangible
results or situations where your angel's assistance has aided you: "So
far this month, I have _____." Once you are done, move on to the
remainder of the month.

October 21

Today your angel is asking you to be grateful that something in your life has
come to an end. A cycle has finished, or the journey you have been taking has
put you at your final destination. Endings abound today, and it is important to
be grateful for them. It is natural for things to come to an end. Completion is
an important part of living. Without endings, there can be no beginnings. Pay
attention today, as your finishing energy may not be as obvious as you think.
It might be something you didn't know was coming to a stop. As you become
aware of each ending, take a breath and say thank you. It doesn't matter what it
is or where you are, just use your breathwork in conjunction with your gratitude
practice. The two together allow the old energy to blow away while creating
space for something new to seed. We thank the seasons and the year, so now it is
time to find all the other endings to be thankful for today.

October 22

Today, your angel wants you to be grateful for all the people who push your but-
tons, ruffle your feathers, and get under your skin. These people are your teachers of contrast, reflecting to you all the things you do not want. How incredible
it is that these individuals offered themselves to you as mirrors. Every time they
appear, space is created for you to let the Divine know what you *do* want, not
what you *don't* want. What do you really, truly want, from the top of your head
to the tips of your toes? What do you cry for in your prayers? All those annoying
people in your life are merely a reminder that you still have some manifesting

to do, so be grateful for them because they won't be around once you finally get what you want.

October 23

There are some constants in our world that many of us take for granted, one of which is that the sun will come up every single day. Yet the act of the sun being able to shine unobstructed and bathe the earth in life-giving light is a blessing. Its light allows us to have food, and the vitamin D it helps humans manufacture builds our immune systems and make our bones strong. The sun plays such a vital part in our daily life. Today, it would be nice to thank it. Consider a morning salutation to the sun and send it waves of gratitude energy. Without the sun, the world as you know it would cease to exist. As you feel the sun kiss your skin while you watch the birds go about their business today, say thank you. As you eat fresh food, say thank you. Those are the gifts of the sun.

October 24

As you move through the world today, your angel would like you to find one thing you would like more of and thank it like you have never been grateful for something before. The more real and sincere gratitude you can send to one thing, the more powerful that energy, which in turn makes it super magnetic. And the more magnetic something is, the more of itself it will attract. That translates to more of it for which you can be grateful. Although this is an incredibly simple process in theory, do not be fooled into thinking it is easy. In order to hold this level of gratitude around one thing you want, you must overcome the mental and emotional blocks of that thing not already being in your life. Your angel wants you to be kind and playful in this game of gratitude—do not beat yourself up if your thoughts stray, and don't be cruel to yourself for feelings of lack. If find yourself slipping, just move quickly into gratitude and hold that space for as long as you can.

October 25

Today it is time to feel grateful for your clothes, all those wonderful garments you wear to protect you from the elements, and even the ones that you bought just because they look amazing on you. Clothes work hard for you: They are worn, washed, dried, and hung in a dark space waiting to be worn again. They show up for you without expecting anything in return. It seems only fair to take a moment and show them a little gratitude and love. You could open your closet and drawers and say a small prayer of thanks, or you could go deeper and thank each item of clothing with the memories they helped create. Or you could write a list of all the ways you are grateful for what's stashed away inside your wardrobe and drawers.

October 26

Yesterday, your angel prompted you to give thanks to your clothes; today it is time to thank your shoes. Out of all the items you decorate your body with, your shoes have the hardest—and sometimes stinkiest—job. If you wear specific footwear for work, start with that: tell it how grateful you are for holding you up, protecting your feet, and making sure you have firm footing in your work environment. Next, focus on your everyday footwear or sports shoes. These shoes really take a pounding and usually have the heaviest use. Thank these shoes for what they do for your feet and what they allow you to do when you wear them. You might even have some fun memories to connect with the gratitude process. Now move on to dress and party shoes. For the most part, these types of shoe are worn the most infrequently, so I usually thank them for their patience. Make sure every pair of shoes you own is blessed with gratitude. They work hard and deserve to be acknowledged.

October 27

If you use a mode of transportation to get around—be it the bus, your own car, the train, your bike, or even an Uber—today is the day to be grateful for your mobility. There is freedom in being able to get from one place to another. We get a sense of personal autonomy and power when we know we have the capacity to do things on our own and whenever we want, yet we all forget to be grateful for this. Mobility, travel, and even driving to the store are gifts. So when you get into your car or find your seat on public transport today, your angels wants you to say thank you. You have the freedom to move. Honor your chariot by sending a wave of gratitude over it. Love it up in a real and honest way. When you think about all the places you can visit and the things you get to do, how could you not be deeply grateful?

October 28

Today, your angel would like you to spend time giving thanks to all the appliances in your home. As you do so, say out loud all the things this appliance gifts you. Your fridge gives you the ability to keep and store fresh food for extended periods of time. Your washing machine gives you the gift of clean clothes. Your dryer blesses you with warm, fluffy clothes. Your kettle boils your water, allowing you to have coffee or tea. Your stove gives the gift of being able to make cake (okay, it makes more than cake, but cake is a pretty amazing gift). The angels and I think you understand where we are taking these examples. Walk around your house and start listing your appliances with at least one reason you are so grateful to have it in your life. This form of gratitude connects you to the items you own, giving them more purpose than just as "stuff" you own.

October 29

Today, angel Chana wants you to be grateful for the trees. Even if you don't personally consider yourself a tree person, trees are so important to the human experience on planet Earth. They help keep the air breathable and are part of the planet's respiratory system. Can you imagine how your body would work without your lungs? It is easy to look at trees and forget the balance they create in the physical ecosystem. It is important that we do not only feel grateful once they are all gone. Instead, being grateful for them now will allow us a future that will still have trees in it. Find one thing, just one, that you can honestly say you are grateful for that a tree provides you while it is living happily in the ground. Then the next time you pass a tree, say thank you and carry on.

October 30

Each morning when I do my own personal gratitude list, I always give thanks for coffee. I know it seems strange, but you may have noticed one of the big themes the angels have made you focus on this month is to reconnect to the reasons you buy, consume, and own certain things. Even though I only have one cup a day, I really love coffee. But I am so grateful for that one cup, that it makes it onto my gratitude list every single morning. So what beverage are you truly grateful for, and what feelings come your way when you drink it? My coffee warms me up on a cold morning and slowly but surely brings my brain online for the rest of the day. It also tastes amazing. Now it's your turn: love it up with your favorite beverage!

October 31

It seems fitting to end this month by making a list of all the things you have been grateful for over the course of the month. I know, more lists; even though the angels and I said this wasn't just about lists, the truth is that a list makes things visible. So please, indulge us. You may have learned some new things or found a new sense of appreciation for old things. Either way, by now you should have a pretty healthy list of things to be incredibly grateful for in your everyday life. Now is the time to make a list of everything. Do this slowly and in a way that feels more like you are honoring this list rather than surrounding it with the energy of yet another task. Allow the energy of gratitude to flow over you and soak it up as much as possible.

Closing Ceremony for the Month

Your time with angel Chana has now come to an end, for this year anyway. It is time to pack up your altar for the angel of gratitude. Even if you are going to continue some of the gratitude practices you have learned this month, it is important to clear away your altar for now as a way of closing the energy you have been working with over the past month. Wash your magical items, wipe down your altar surface, and put any cards or images away. Remember to wave a smoking herb bundle over the space to cleanse the energy and reset it, making it ready for the next angel. As you clean and reset your altar, say a small prayer of thanks:

> *Angel Chana, I thank thee*
> *For showing me once again*
> *All the goodness that surrounds me*
> *From big to small*
> *Blessing are all around me*
> *You have moved me from mundane to magic*
> *In a month of thanks*
> *I am grateful*
> *For you*

For all that makes my life worth living
For now, I clean and clear this sacred workspace
This altar I cleanse
To honor you
To honor the work we have done.
Thank you.

Chapter Twelve
NOVEMBER

Sophia
The Angel of Reflection

Welcome to November, the month of reflection. This was an interesting chapter to write; unlike the others, the angel Sophia really wanted me to experience the lesson and teachings she had to share. I guess you could say this chapter was more of an immersive experience. What it will be for you, however, only you will know—and you won't know until after you have traversed it, which is, well, a reflection. Throughout this month, your angel is going to give you lessons, messages, and guidance on reflections that could take the form of instructional tasks to ground the lesson. The meditations, observations, or sometimes the guidance itself may be more abstract, as it is channeled material. Just know that whatever you personally receive from the daily prompt is correct and valid. You will learn a lot more about what a reflection is, what it is not, how to use it for healing, and when to leverage it for manifestation. There is so much more in the days of this month than you could possibly ever imagine when it comes to the energy of reflection. You might even find yourself peering into mirrors, trying to water scry, or even contemplating lessons past. What is and is not could get very twisted inside this particular chapter of mirrors. Just know that angel Sophia always has your best interests at heart. She wants you to find joy, feel love, and be at peace with your daily experience. Hold on to that knowledge as you make your way through November.

Connection Prayer: Bringing in the Energy of the Angel of Reflection

To get the most out of your month with the angel Sophia, set up your November altar. For your altar this month, you will need physical objects that are reflective: mirrors, crystals, water, objects with surfaces that allow you to see things in them. I also suggest leaving space on your altar to add things as you move through your month. Once you have your altar cleansed and set up, light your candle. This month I recommend using silver or white candles, as they represent the energy of the reflection. When you are ready to light your candle, say the following prayer to bring in the energy of angel Sophia and connect them to your November:

Angel Sophia, I summon thee;
Hold the mirror toward me
Make me see
The parts I often ignore
Moments I may have forgotten
Flashes of inspiration that catch the light
Move through me.
Let me be the reflection
Of the Divine
Of grace
Of miracles.
Show me how to read the light
How to swim in the deep waters
Ripples of imagination
Waves of memories.
Sophia, I call thee
Binding you to my November
Stay with me this month
Guide me
Hold me close as we move
From one journey to the next
And so it is.

Messages for the Days of the Month

November 1

When most people hear the word "reflection," they tend to conjure images of the past; looking back somehow goes hand in hand with this word. But what if your angel told you that isn't the case? We want you to open up to the possibility that reflections can be very much about the here and now, and they can indeed foreshadow what is about to manifest in your future. Sometimes a reflection is right in front of you, mirrored to you by the people in your life. As you begin your work with reflections this month, start by being aware of where they show up in your day. Is it a memory from the past? Perhaps a real mirror or a passing window? Maybe it is just seeing the emotion in another's face. Just for today, raise your awareness of where places for reflections exist in your life. Creating a map for the month is going to make this journey much more enjoyable.

November 2

Sometimes a reflection is a recurring sign: a message, a symbol, a piece of music that seems to pop up again and again. The sign is an answer, a message, and reflective energy. As you move through your tasks today, be on the lookout for repeating signs. Something has been trying to get your attention and needs you to honor its presence now. This sign may not make sense to you right away, and that is perfectly okay; just take note of it. Write down what you've observed and allow the path of understanding to unfold. It might take a little while to fully appreciate what is being sent to you and how it is relevant for you right now. But the more you just surrender and allow, the more will become clear. Your angel is here to assist, so remember to ask for additional clarity if you need to.

November 3

All queries are answered by divine consciousness, yet we may not always be aware because they often show up in the people around us. These people reflect the answer to you in a very exciting way: look for answers that may be hidden in conversations and the exchange of ideas as you process their words. As you move through today, be on the lookout for those who are offering up an answer or solution to a question or problem you have been seeking some sort of resolution around. Remember they have been sent to you intentionally. Your angel has placed them on your path to serve as the answer you seek, but reflection is needed on your part.

November 4

There are times when looking back and observing the past is a very positive action. When you can identify how far you have come and how differently you respond to the circumstances around you, you can observe growth as both a person and a spirit. All humans expand and move closer to alignment with the energy of their soul, and some do it faster than others. Neither is better or worse, only different. Today, your angel would like you to find an area in your life in which you know you have grown. Identify where in your journey that growth changed and became more soulful, and honor that energy. Who you are today in this moment is a reflection of that part of your past. This is a sacred moment: bless it and allow the unfolding to continue.

November 5

Today your angel wants you to pick an emotion that is noticeable and easily detected as you move about the day. Once you have your emotion selected, think about how you embody that emotion. By this the angels mean how you stand, speak, and act while riding the wave of this particular emotion. Now go forth and find this emotional state in the people, conversations, and activities you engage in today. The world is a giant mirror, and this task is to illustrate just how much power you have in bending reality to reflect how you feel. Evidence to support the emotion you have chosen to embody will be everywhere, especially now that you are on the lookout for it. All you have to do is be a seeker, looking for yourself and your emotional state in all those around, in all that you see, touch, and smell. Your human experience truly is a magical one.

November 6

There have been times in your life where a reflection has been a foreshadowing, a glimpse into a future that is yet to be lived. Today is one of those days. Your future self is working hard to send you a message that you are on the right path and headed in the right direction—all is working out exactly the way it is meant to. The message could arrive as a déjà vu moment. It could appear in a conversation. Or you might even look in the mirror and see your future self staring back at you. These glimpses into what could be if you stay on track are all around you today. Your angels have been listening to you and want you to see first-hand what is in the process of creating itself. The angels understand that humans sometimes need to see some proof in order to fully trust the manifestation process.

November 7

Today your angel has something fun for you to try: get a bowl of any size and shape and fill it about halfway with water. Next, on a piece of paper, write: "How will my angel move me today?" Place that piece of paper under your bowl of water. Take a few slow breaths and imagine the answer to your question reflected on the water's surface. Keep in mind this is meant to be fun; do not worry if you get to the end of the day and feel like you weren't able to make this work. Your angels want to activate your imagination and your throat, so speak what first comes to mind. Open your mouth and talk it out loud—you might even say "this is so silly," and that's perfectly fine. Remember, too, that what you see might not necessarily be visual: you might receive a feeling or inner knowing. Do not dismiss anything; speak it. Perhaps you will see a flash of light or a color dancing across the surface of the water; speak this out loud as well. If you get nothing at all, that is absolutely fantastic. Open your imagination a little wider and remember that this is a game and there are no prizes at the end. Have fun and, most importantly, imagine.

November 8

Looking back over your week or your day can be a great way to show yourself how much progress you have made toward a goal. As you reflect on the actions and decisions you made over the last seven days or twenty-four hours, write out how many of those were taken in order to move the needle on your current goal. If you are working on your health, write down all the times you made healthy decisions. If you have money-related goals, think about all the smart choices you made. If you are currently focused on love, list all the ways you showed yourself love and how open you were to receiving it. If your current goals are more career-focused, make a list of all the things you did to enhance your career or grow your business. The more you do this exercise, the more progress you will see. This, in turn, will create positive momentum in your life. This is a very powerful way to use the energy of reflection.

November 9

Today your angel is asking you to see if you can find moments in your past where your life branched off and went in a different direction. Think of those crossroads moments where you could have gone one way but chose another. There was a reason behind that decision, and your angel would like you to explore if that reason is still relevant today. If it is not, how can you change direction again? For the most part, we keep directing energy toward past decisions. This not only disconnects us from the here and now but also drains our energy: we feel like we don't have enough time, money, or energy to make different decisions and forge new paths into our future. If the decision you made is not one you would make today, change it. And if it is, reaffirm why. It is important to connect your reason to the present and see how it will shape the future. The power of reflection is that it can and does drive us.

November 10

We live in a unique moment in history: never before have we, as a species, lived in an age where we see ourselves so frequently. We are everywhere, constantly being reflected to ourselves. Every single person has a camera in their pockets. Videos, reels, and posts constantly show pieces of ourselves to the outside world. Today your angel asks you: Do you like what you see? Are the pieces of you out in the world reflecting a you that you are happy with and that truly reflects who you are on the inside? The upside of us seeing ourselves so often is we have more opportunities to shift, self-correct, and change course when we see something we aren't overjoyed with. And though we are not talking cosmetics here, reflection might include seeing how much light, love, and joy radiates from us when we talk about something we love. Your angels say to soak in reflections that show your light. Amplify and send more of that light into the world.

CHECK-IN ONE

It has now been ten days since you started working with the angel Sophia and the theme of reflections. Now is the ideal time to visit your altar and consider if the items you set it up with are still relevant or if you might need to switch them out or add to them. It is also time to give your altar space a bit of a clean, freshen up any cut flowers, and light your candles once more. Say a small prayer or mantra, or sit in silent meditation for a couple of minutes. This small journey to your altar will bring your mind, body, and soul back to a place of devotion and center you in the theme of the month.

November 11

Do you remember the moment right after you finished reading a good book? It's that feeling of resolution where you know that all the pieces have come together but you aren't sure what to do next except lean into sharing the book with others. That feeling is the power of reflection, in its emotional form. A feeling has moved through you and nudges you into some sort of action. The memories swirl in your mind and leave a space for questions, sparks of inspiration, and a desire to talk about what has been stirred inside you. This is the power of a good book: it holds a mirror to your soul and asks you what you see and how it feels. Today, your angel asks: have you read any good books lately?

November 12

Take a moment today to look at the technological world that is always at your fingertips. Technology can do one of two things: feed your mind with fear and sadness or wrap you in waves of joy and abundance. Optimistic people tend to follow only other joyful people, not in a toxic-positivity way, but in a way that shows even in a world of pain, there will always be love, kindness, and compassion. The so-called realists among you tend to follow what causes anxiety and worry. Your angel wants you to start being a lot more deliberate with the way you allow technology to brainwash you. Right here and now, ask yourself what vibrational feeling you want to have every time you check your phone, log in to your computer, or even watch TV. Then, make sure that only the people, pictures, videos, and sounds which reflect that feeling back to you are what you see. This practice isn't encouraging ignorance or denying reality—it allows you to choose how you wish to engage with the content your mind and heart are absorbing.

November 13

In many respects, success is a reflection. It is not something you can pinpoint while traversing through it. You can only see it after the fact in the rearview mirror of your life. Yet so many people strive for it as if it is a destination: they set goals and wait for a big billboard in the sky that says "Congratulations, you made it!" to light up. Success is something you notice only once you have passed it—ironic, isn't it? Today your angel is asking you to take a good hard look in the rearview mirror and see when and where you passed success. It is more than likely hanging out with the last goal you accomplished or the last time you felt good about a relationship, your body, your job, or maybe the last time you got out of bed and put on pants. Success is back there, in the way behind.

November 14

There will be times during your day where you will wonder if you are in the right place at the right time doing the right thing. We all have moments where we wonder if we are making the right decisions or if our lives are going in the right direction. Your angel wants you to understand that the answer to these questions is more about trust than fact. Trust that you are being intentional with your life, and that your decisions are the right ones. Trust that the opportunities coming to you now are aligned with the dreams you have. This is where your future reflections will meet your past reflections and merge at the current moment. Flashes of what could be and what has been will assist you in creating what is now. The more you trust, the clearer these points of reflection will be. Instead of asking when and how, today, lean into trust and see what magic you can create.

November 15

There may be a moment today that takes you back in time to a place and space not as joyful as the one you are in right now. This memory is not returning to bring you down; it is floating forward wrapped in a blanket of deep, lasting gratitude for your ability to make different decisions and take your life in a different direction. Humans tend to not allow themselves to think too deeply on how difficult it is to do things differently. Making new decisions with unknown consequences can be quite scary. But today, as you reflect on this memory and all the feelings that come with it, you will see just how gratifying it is to do things differently. It may not have been easy to get where you are today, but this reflection can show you just how grateful you are that you made it. Well done, you!

November 16

There is magic living inside your bathroom mirror that has the ability to show you who you are and what you are capable of. For some reason when most people look into it, they are only looking for flaws or to see if they have covered their imperfections artfully. Yet who you are in the mirror—naked, raw, and bare—is the magical version of you, the version that holds all the power. Each and every day, your most potent and magnetic self is being reflected back at you—flawless, pure, and powerful. Today your angel wants you to see if it is possible to accept this reflection of yourself. Look in your reflection's eyes and see that burning light of creation staring right back at you, giving you all you need to make today the best day you have ever experienced—well, for now, anyway.

November 17

There are multiple versions of you within the dimensional matrix known as time and space. One of them is the perfect reflection of the life you are working to create. One of your many versions is reaching across the multiverse toward you to activate the codes and energies required for you to create your dream life, to attract, maintain, and sustain the life you see in your meditation. Dream about it in your sleep and hold it in the deepest parts of your heart. This version of you is a mirror that shows you that what you seek is not only possible, you are already living it. Today, open yourself to receive the energy from this version of yourself. Listen to the whispers. Follow the nudges. Trust the inner knowing. That which moves you today is you.

November 18

Light can be created in one of two ways: generated from a source or reflected. You can use light both ways, too. You can create it yourself (the more desirable option) or reflect others' light into the world. The latter is a worthy action but only if what you are reflecting is what you want to truly share with the world. For the most part, humans reflect the light of the brightest people around them and dim themselves in order to fit in. This in turn leads to reflecting light that is not authentic to the self or aligned to your true nature and beliefs. Today, your angel wants you to take notice of whose light you are allowing to bounce off you and where you are dimming in order to allow someone else to shine. This level of awareness will allow you to be more aligned with the light within and around you.

November 19

Today your angel is nudging you ever so gently to allow others to see a piece of you that you tend to keep hidden. Think of a small fragment of yourself that for whatever reason you have been reluctant to let shine. Your angel wants you to do your best to reveal it and see how others reflect that light back to you. One of the reasons you have been so scared to share this part of yourself is fear of how those around you will respond, but are you sure that others will have a negative reaction to your light being seen? Fear loves to create monsters where there are none and create images inside your head that don't truly reflect what is happening. Today, trust that you can let more of your light out. Slowly and gently, release your light and yourself into the world and hold space for the positive reactions of others to seeing you shine brighter.

November 20

There are moments in all our lives where we have desperately wanted one thing but its opposite turned up instead. In these instances, the mind is not reflecting what the eyes want to see. In other words, your thoughts and feelings are not a match for your desires. Your mind is an amazing mirror that constantly reflects to you what your true inner beliefs are. You might not like what you see, but that does not mean they aren't true. Today, your angel is asking you to monitor your thoughts to see if you can change one or two to realign yourself with the results you want to see. Remember that thoughts create feelings, and feelings create the conditions you move through every day. You will know when enough of your thoughts and feelings are on board—you will start to see things with your eyes that match the desires in your heart.

CHECK-IN TWO

You have now had twenty days working with your theme of reflections and your angel Sophia. It is time to pull out your journal and see how the prompts have been helping you stay in the energy of reflection. Starting with the following prompt, make lists of tangible results or situations where your angel's assistance has aided you: "So far this month, I have_____." Once you are done, move on to the remainder of the month.

November 21

Today we want to discuss time, the one thing that really isn't well-measured by clocks or calendars. Sure, both are great ways to mark the days' beginning and end, but they aren't the best way to look at time as it affects your life. For the most part, people overestimate what they can do in a short period of time, like a month or a year, and underestimate what they can do in a longer period, such as three months or five years. Today your angel is asking you to think about everything you've done in a three-month block and see how far you have traveled in the last five years. This reflection on change and growth will give you a much better indicator on what you have achieved in your life than beating yourself up for not hitting goals set at the beginning of the year. Time is very much a reflective device; when used correctly, can be an incredible vehicle to see how well your life is truly going.

November 22

You have been working with reflections for a while now, so you have a better understanding of how they show up in your day and can teach lessons. For this reason, your angel wants you to do a little experiment today: All you need to do is have a positive thought that you keep coming back to throughout the day—it's that simple. You can even set an alert on your phone every thirty minutes that signals you to hold that positive thought for at least sixty seconds. At the end of the day, all you have to do is see how holding onto this thought changed or shifted the way your day unfolded. This reflection on how positive thoughts can create positive energy in your life will show you yet again how reflections are working in your life and create a reality in which you flow.

November 23

Did you know that you cannot find something to love and appreciate in another person unless it lives in you? When you look at others and admire how they glow and shine, you are doing so from a place of reflection. When you see a loved one and feel the energy of love pump through you, it is because you are engaging in the reflection of your own love. When something delights and pleases you, it is because it is acting from a place of reflection. You can't love, adore, and appreciate something without it first being inside you. For this reason, the angels say that you are and have always been complete and whole. No matter what storm clouds move through your mind or how your emotions churn, at the end of the day you are love, beauty, brilliance, and light. If you weren't, you would not be able to identify and find it in others.

November 24

Today your angel would like you to reflect on how you react when things go well in your life. When the good vibes start to roll and gather momentum, do you sink into the energy they create and roll with them? Or do you pick fights, get angry and resentful, and find yourself slipping into old patterns of behavior? How you act when this energy is around reflects how you feel about abundance and, more to the point, how much abundance you can have and for how long. When people have a negative reaction to things going well in their lives, what they are reflecting is a belief that this energy is limited, that it will be gone soon, so there's no point to enjoying it. This attitude typically leads to anger and resentment. The ability to relax and ride the wave, on the other hand, shows an understanding of the fact that you are in the flow of your own divine supply—so be aware and observe how you and those around you act or react to good vibes and flowing abundance.

November 25

Your angel has spoken at great length this month about how the world outside you is nothing more than a screen onto which you project your strongest thoughts and feelings. Today, your angel wants you to start deliberately setting up new thoughts and new feelings so you can manifest a new world. For this choose-your-own-adventure, select one area of life where you really would like to see changes. It could be your health, relationships, finances, or even your job. Open your journal or note-taking app on your phone and start writing about how you want to feel and think about this area of your life. You may not be thinking and feeling that way now, and that's okay. Just write about how you do want to feel, the thoughts you want to have, and get it on paper or on your screen. Repeat this daily until some of these new feelings and thoughts start to appear in your life. Start being deliberate with your projections and the world will start reflecting a new reality right before your eyes.

November 26

Let's talk about using reflections for deliberate daily intention-setting around money. Before you start work, leave the house, or head into your daily chores, stop for a moment, close your eyes and visualize how you want to feel, think, and act regarding your money. As you visualize, find the mirror in your mind that reflects the image of the reality you wish to create. Find yourself in that reflected scene and hold your reflection's gaze. Let the energy pass between you for around two minutes and then allow the image to fade. Take some slow, deep breaths and go about your business as usual. If you feel you need to, you can connect back with that internal mirror throughout the day.

November 27

Today your angel wants you to focus on setting up a reflection of your health that you would like to create or inevitably see in your outside world. To do this, your angel would like you to sit in meditation for a couple of minutes and visualize how your future healthy, happy, and content self would move through their day. What actions would they take? What thoughts would they have? Command this image to embed in your mind and slowly come out of your meditative state. Now, create a vision board based on the feelings, thoughts, and images from that visualization. This vision board does not have to be big; it can be half of a sheet of regular printer paper (8.5" x 11"). Just make sure that none of the images overhang the sides and do not feature words. Once your vision board is complete, find somewhere to place it that you will see it every day. What you've created is your new mirror of health and well-being that is going to reflect to you what you want so you can attain your goal.

November 28

As you move through your day and interact with people, think about how you want to be treated. Consider for a moment how you would like to engage with both people you know and people you do not. Move through your day as if you are already living the sort of experience you wish to create with others. Each time you encounter someone, treat them in the way you wish to be treated, even if they do not respond as you would like. Do your best to not have expectations around others' responses as you go about the day, and instead, stay focused on what *you* are doing and how you want to eventually feel. Use yourself as the reflection: act, feel, think, and move as if you are instructing the world without telling or judging. By the end of the day, something magical may occur, and it won't be because of anyone else—it will only be a result of how you now feel about yourself.

November 29

When you can't seem to get a grip on your day and time seems to march on by without any real tasks being accomplished, it is a sign that your mind is racing and restless. When the mind is in chaos, constantly jumping from one random thought to the next, your outer world will reflect it. This happens to everyone more often than you might think, and even to those you may consider high achievers. It's good news, because now you can see that it can change and shift to something more helpful and fulfilling. When you notice that your mind is all over the place, simply stop yourself for a moment. Find a quiet place to sit. Take a few slow, deep breaths, and if it is safe, close your eyes and connect to the energy of the day. See yourself moving through it, getting things done, and feeling accomplished. Then get up and get on with it. This quick reflective moment can and will change the entire feel and flow of your day.

November 30

There is a feeling at this time of year about how we want to see the world and the desire to give back. As you move closer to the holiday season, whatever that holiday is for you personally, you might find yourself questioning humanity and your place in it. Keep in mind everything you have learned in this chapter and that reflections work both ways: How you feel will often show up as what you see, and what you see can change how you feel. The world outside you is constantly bouncing light and imagery off of the world inside you in an exchange of energy that creates your lived experience. As you move into this time of year and start a larger reflection on life, the year, and what you have done with your time on the planet, just remember, you can always choose to feel differently, just like you can always choose to seek out other things to focus on and see. You have choice and choice is powerful. Make a different choice and your life will ultimately reflect a different experience. The power is in you and all around you.

Closing Ceremony for the Month

Your time with angel Sophia has now come to an end, for this year anyway. It is time to pack up your altar for the angel of reflection. Wash your magical items, wipe down your altar surface, pour out any water you were using, and cleanse your crystals before putting them away. Remember to wave a smoking herb bundle over the space so that you can cleanse the energy and reset it, making it ready for the next angel. As you clean and reset your altar, say a small prayer of thanks:

Angel Sophia, I thank thee
For guiding me
Using me as a vessel for your lessons
Teaching me through others
And holding space for me to see
My eyes have been opened anew
Reflections of myself and my life surround me
I will not look at the world the same
Nor will I question my role as a creator
Thank you for your time, Angel of Reflections
For now, I clean and clear this sacred workspace
This altar I cleanse
To honor you
To honor the work we have done.
Thank you.

Chapter Thirteen
DECEMBER

Lailah
The Angel of Darkness

Welcome to December, the month of darkness. If you have read from January, the very beginning, welcome to the end of your journey with the angels. If you are starting here or only halfway through your journey, welcome to the darkness. There is much to learn. Throughout this month your angel is going to give you lessons, messages, and guidance about darkness that could take the form of instructional tasks to ground the lesson. The meditations, observations, and sometimes the guidance itself may be more abstract, as it is channeled material. Just know that whatever you personally receive from the daily prompt is correct and valid. You might think this is an odd theme for angels to be teaching, that darkness is the opposite energy to what you believe the angels should be teaching. It is exactly for this reason the angels feel it is necessary to end with darkness. The angels do not view darkness the same way humans do—they see it as a miraculous space, an energy that births all things into creation, a portal to the light that everything seems to seek. Angel Lailah has thus stepped forward to deliver your lessons this month and walk with you as you learn the magic and mysteries of the dark. Perhaps you will dispel some of the fears about being in the dark and maybe even move to a point of inviting the darkness into your life intentionally.

Connection Prayer: Bringing in the Energy of the Angel of Darkness

To get the most out of your month with the angel Lailah, set up your December altar. If you have black crystals, use them this month to anchor your altar. Think about putting some tarot cards such as the Moon, the Star, and the Hermit on your altar as your darkness committee. Lastly, consider including some black feathers to represent your angel of darkness. As always, I suggest leaving space on your altar to add things to it as you move through your month. Once you have your altar cleansed and set up, light your candle. I recommend black for the candle color this month to best represent the energy of darkness, and I encourage you to use birthday candles to symbolize the darkness as not permanent; some of the lessons in this chapter will remind you how fleeting it can be. When you are ready to light your candle, say the following prayer to bring in the energy of angel Lailah and connect her to your December:

Angel Lailah, I summon thee
To keep me safe
To protect me
Guide me through the darkness
Teach me how to see
With night eyes.
Void of light
Through mountains
Over streams
A life in the dark
Make it magical
Show me
How to move through my fear
Leave my doubts
On the floor
As darkness comes
Knocking at the door.
Angel Lailah, I bind thee
To this month
Absent of light

To my calendar and these days
Keep my hand in yours
For this journey
In you I trust
This candle our only light
Let the fun commence.
And so it is.

Messages for the Days of the Month

December 1

There is magic in the dark—it is a sacred space away from prying eyes that grants us moments where the noise just drops away. This is not a place where fear lives, but where the soul lives. All pieces of the self begin and end in the darkness of the universe. If it was not for the darkness, you would not be able to burst forth into the light. Your angel Lailah wants you to find the safe spaces in your life today, the quiet places, the moments and gaps where you can stop, drop your shoulders, and unclench your jaw. This is the magic of the dark and the opportunity it gives you. This is also the place where Spirit communes with you—it is easier for it to be heard. Listen for the whispers, feel for nudges, and lean into the knowing, for the darkness is opening a portal to miracles this month. All you need to do is step inside.

December 2

Darkness is a natural part of your human experience. It is why you have day and night, summer and winter. This contrast is important for your energetic, emotional, and mental well-being. Equal parts rest and stillness are needed for active and social energy. It seems easier to always be switched on, especially into your constantly humming technological world. Today your angel is asking you to see where you can bring more of the energy of the darkness into your day. Where could you be quieter? Where could you create more space to pause and take a breath before acting or allowing yourself to slip into reactionary energy? Write these prompts into your journal and create a list that you can follow through with during your day.

December 3

Darkness brings with it a different perspective, a new way to look at things that you take for granted. When the lights go out and only the outlines remain, you can see things simply. Everything is reduced to shapes, lines, and blocks of light or dark. This level of vision allows you to see that all things can be seen differently or in a new way, different from your expectations. Today your angel would like you to bring this reduced visibility to your daily experience, especially to places and situations where you might be reading too much into things. Strip the story away, block out the details, and reduce everything to shapes and outlines. If you could see this situation through the lens of darkness, how would it appear? Nothing looks the same in the dark as it does in the light. This softening may be exactly what you need right now to keep it simple and clarify what comes next.

December 4

There are times when darkness feels a lot like healing; these times are when you feel like you need to shut the world out, go inward, and focus your energy on yourself. You could be in physical recovery or suffering from loss or another emotional wound. Your angel Lailah wants you to know that there is no time limit on how long you stay in this space. Society tends to want everyone to move quickly through their healing phases. People around you might seem impatient with your need to stay inside the darkness, but do not allow their fear to stop you from healing in the way your soul knows you need to heal. Your angel is standing in the darkness with you, bathing you in the energy of unconditional love. They will always hold this healing for you and never ask you to rush or move before you are ready.

December 5

Darkness can feel a lot like peace, especially when we have more time to wind down and less time to run about. There is something beautiful about having more dark than light in our life for a season; it forces us to compact our activity into short bursts of time and energy. At the same time, we open more space to simply be, settle down, and even sleep. As you make your way through your daily tasks today, think about how you can compact that list. How can you shorten the amount of activity today so that you can create more peace? See how you can condense your time spent doing and allow more space and opportunity for being. Less busy, more silly. Today, darkness offers you the invitation of peace—peace of mind, peace of body, and peace of soul.

December 6

Darkness isn't a happy place for everyone; in fact, it can be quite anxiety-ridden for some. The angels want you to know that regardless of how the dark moves you, you are safe in its embrace. Your angel of darkness wants you to start thinking of being in the dark as being enclosed in the wings of your personal protection angel, wrapped in purpose and love. We also know it can feel scary if you are not used to feeling these raw emotions; being completely swept up in this level of love can terrify some, but that just makes the angels want to love you more. So ease into the darkness on your own terms—slowly let it creep around you, absorb your pain, and bathe you in nothing but the purest love. Gently embrace more of the dark as your heart heals. This is an act of trust—we promise not to break it.

December 7

Entering the dark is a sacred act. It asks you to let go of the need to shine and be seen. In the dark there is just you. There is no one to prop you up or tear you down. You can be vulnerable; no one else's gaze will touch you. The only critic in the room will be yourself. It is in the dark you can embrace who and what you are, the self you alone have created. The dark offers a space of acceptance in which there are no judgments, which means that you alone get to decide if you can look yourself in the eyes and say "I love you," or if rejection is all you have to offer. Here, the angel of darkness offers you the sacred gift of compassion. Regardless of how you see yourself, your angels will always view your being as divine, complete, and worthy of unconditional love.

December 8

The darkness does not have to be physical: it can be a mood, a feeling, or even a state of mind. The darkness can move, morph, and shift through all parts of your life. Today, notice where darkness is making itself known and see if you can figure out what message it is sending you. Is it coming to this part of your experience to nudge you into rest? Could it be alerting you to a need to be more vulnerable? You will be amazed at how your angel uses the darkness to send you subtle messages about your current state of affairs. You just need to shift your awareness to notice and understand them. You may even notice a part of your life that is itself a period of darkness. Think about exploring why that is and what lessons your angel could be setting you up to learn. Remember to come to these moments as an adventurer exploring what is possible, not casting judgment. This perspective allows you to assess and act rather than hook and get stuck.

December 9

You only know that light exists because of dark—in the contrast of darkness, the light is made visible. It shines brightly and can guide you in certain directions. When there is nothing but light all around you, it is difficult to see any path. We can get lost, confused, and lack direction. Only in darkness can you clearly see the journey the light carves out for you; it travels through the void of darkness. The darkness is important because it can move, direct, and show you the path of your soul's journey. It provides the blank page on which the light can write: the story of you spelled out on a black background, like stars mapped in the sky that help you navigate. What an incredible blessing the darkness is.

December 10

Sometimes darkness feels a lot like pain, whether physical or emotional. There is no doubt that when the physical, mental, and emotional bodies are in pain, it is hard to see the light. The darkness of existence presses in and seems to block everything else out. The angels call this a state of protection, during which they wrap their wings tightly around you as you let go, release, and bring the pain body into alignment with the well-being body. Pain brings us a contrast that shows us in brilliant color what being free of pain looks like, a place outside the protection of the angel's wings. Your angel would like you to meditate on what your life could look like if there was no pain it. What would it be like if the things that once hurt you suddenly lost their charge and effect? Knowing you are wrapped in protection today means you can explore this area of your life safely.

CHECK-IN ONE

It has now been ten days since you started working with the angel Lailah and the theme of darkness. Now is the ideal time to visit your altar and consider if the items you set it up with are still relevant or if you need to switch them out or add to them. It is also time to give your altar space a bit of a clean, freshen up any cut flowers, and light your candles once more. Say a small prayer or mantra, or sit in silent meditation for a couple of minutes. This small journey to your altar will bring your mind, body, and soul back to a place of devotion and center you in the theme of the month.

December 11

Darkness can feel a lot like freedom, allowing you to express who you are in your wildest and rawest form. When limits and boundaries are dissolved, the self can be liberated. Today your angel of darkness is asking you to locate this space in your current life, the space where you can drop everything the outside world wants of you. In this space, you get to be the untamed version of yourself. Even if it doesn't look dark, this is a space of darkness and a safe space in which you can relax and restore. If you notice you do not have this kind of space in your life right now, know that you are being called to create one. The size, shape, and place for this space is entirely up to you. For the most part, it is emotive in nature. Feel into it and let the darkness guide you.

December 12

Sometimes darkness feels a lot like fear—not necessarily paralyzing fear or even dread, but fear that stands on the brink of excitement. It is a step before we launch into doing something new, something elevating that has the potential to move you into a new reality. This is a wild space, raw and filled with unknowns. Everything looks and feels different here; nothing is as it seems. We are truly viewing this moment through the lens of darkness, which means darkness is not just an experience or a state of being—it can also be a way in which we view the world, a form of perception. As you move through your day, notice where you are seeing the world through the threshold of fear and excitement. Open your senses to explore this vision as it appears through this lens. This experience, this feeling, this moment is shifting how you think about darkness and how it shows up in your life.

December 13

When you were a child there were times you played in the dark: making shadow puppets, cooking food and singing songs around a campfire were fun moments in the dark. You didn't think about the fact that the sun was not shining; you just looked for ways to entertain yourself. The dark has a way of bringing out the more playful, childlike sides of ourselves. If you allow it, the dark can open up a world of creative energy. Make up stories and characters to imagine into being. Your angel nudges you to let your inner child out to explore and play in the shadows. Sing and dance by the firelight and tell stories that were once only figments of your imagination.

December 14

There are going to be times when the darkness is not yours, when you have to hold space for darkness for others. The more comfortable you get with the darkness yourself, the more others will seek you out to help them do the same. It's not because they are having emotional dark moments in their lives but because they want to learn how to use the energy to balance and restore their own lives. Today, your angel is asking you to be available to others who may have questions about bringing more darkness into their lives. Consider how you will answer questions around discovery and exploration of the dark, and how you will hold space for those who really need to embrace the quiet healing energy the dark can and does bring. We often hear about people being the light and showing others how to do the same, so today we're flipping that narrative and holding space for those exhausted as a result of being constantly "on" and burning for way too long without a rest.

December 15

In many respects, darkness is a promise that can only be delivered in a world of contrast. The dark cannot promise the light if you don't live in a space where this sort of contrast exists. The world you live in is full of contrast, opposing elements, and paradoxes. The dark reminds you that contrast can be a good thing—it means nothing ever stays the same and that things change. Wherever there is one energy, the promise of its opposite is always there. Today your angel is asking you to make a note in your journal about contrasting elements in your life right now. It could be related to your relationships, your job, your health, or even your money. Explore these areas as temporary states like darkness, and consider how you would move or shift into their opposite state if that is actually where you want to be.

December 16

In every lunar cycle, the moon goes dark. It enters a phase of darkness deliberately and intentionally. During this darkness, millions of people around the globe come together to honor this natural lunar state, seeing it as a time of restoration, for new beginnings, and a pause to think about what comes next. Your dark moments are not much different than the moons—moments in the dark also offer you the gifts of space, presence of mind, and possibilities. Every day, you get the choice of whether to accept what you see or change it in some way. Just make sure that any changes you make are not due to feeling flawed or powerless. Instead, think about only adding to the brilliance that is already there.

December 17

Darkness can feel a lot like creativity; it wraps you in a soundproof blanket and shuts out the rest of the world so you can just create, explore, and imagine. There is something comforting about being in your very own creative bubble, separate from the outside world yet somehow plugged into all consciousness. Today you might find yourself craving time to write, paint, draw, sing, dance, or to do whatever activity is your creative outlet. Allow this energy to flow through you and block out whatever is not needed or bringing in all that ignites you. Allow this energy to heal you, calm you, and bring you back to center. Let your angel guide you and open you up to receive the blessing of creative flow.

December 18

The moment before the sun breaks above the horizon each morning often seems the darkest; it is my favorite time of day to sit in contemplation with the angels, as it is the very space where a new day full of potential is being birthed into the world. Once the sun is up, the darkness recedes, rests, and allows the light to take over for a while. This graceful dance of sun and moon begins and ends in the dark. Today you may find moments that remind you of this dance, starting in stillness and quiet and ending the same way, with a wave of buzz and activity in between. There is an easy and graceful flow that takes over your tasks of the day. The dark shows us we do not have to push or force anything into being. Instead, the dark illustrates every day how simple and natural movement, manifestation, and magic really are. Relax into the natural flow of your day today and let the dark show you how easy it can be.

December 19

There will be moments in your day and your week where storm clouds will enter your mind and block out your joy. These are natural. Darkness comes in many forms, and it is perfectly fine to have moments in which it brings worry, doubt, or even temporary fear. The trick is to let the clouds float in and out all by themselves without interfering. Allow the feelings to happen, but do not engage with them and dwell on them. These emotions do not need to stay; they can rise and fall all on their own. Think of these moments as you would any other storm: the dark clouds roll in, the wind picks up, it might rain, and then it is gone just as quickly as it came. No one is on the ground trying to hang onto the storm. Yet people do their best to hang on to these stormy emotions, turning them over in their minds again and again. Your lesson of the day is: acknowledge, observe, do not engage.

December 20

Darkness can feel a lot like an old friend, something you can rely on to visit repeatedly. It's an energy you know and at times welcome without a second thought or question about what it may want. This feeling of comfort can be valid regardless of how you are experiencing darkness in your life right now. Darkness is familiar and familiar things tend to bring us comfort, regardless of whether they are harmful or helpful to us. Today your angel wants you to make a list of expectations you have around the darkness in your life, keeping in mind that it could mean any one of the things already discussed in this chapter—or not. These expectations are what keep your experiences identical every time you come into contact with the dark. If you are feeling particularly brave, speak this out loud after you have finished your list: "How about today you surprise me?" and see what happens.

CHECK-IN TWO

You have now had twenty days working with your theme of darkness and your angel Lailah. It is time to pull out your journal and see how the prompts have been helping you stay in the energy of darkness. Starting with the following prompt, make lists of tangible results or situations where your angel's assistance has aided you: "So far this month, I have _____." Once you are done, move on to the remainder of the month.

December 21

Darkness brings with it an ability to measure our light, to see when and where we spark, to observe how we shine, where we shine, and why. It also allows us to test the strength of our light, providing the ultimate backdrop to play and manipulate our light power. In this moment, the darkness is less about the lack of light and more about how much we can harness the power inside of us. Today, use the dark to measure your light. Notice in which situations you burn the brightest. Also be on the lookout for where you tend to protect or dim your light and use darkness as a form of protection. See if you can also find spaces and places to play with your light, pushing and pulling the light and dark to create space, movement, and opportunity in your day. This is all meant to be fun, so do not take your findings too seriously. Just reverse and adjust accordingly.

December 22

As you move through your daily tasks today, Lailah wants you to play with the idea that the dark is where everything is—really, it's true. Out of darkness, space and the universe were birthed. It thus stands to reason that out of that same darkness, your own personal universe is being formed as well. Imagine a giant black hole into which you could reach and pull something you really want. Or think about the dark night sky and imagine that every time a wish is granted, a star lights up. Each manifestation of darkness adds light to the world, so it follows that the more darkness we have, the more room is created for abundance. Have fun with this idea and see how creative you can get.

December 23

Darkness is your most magical transmuting machine. When things in your life feel heavy or daily existence is weighing you down, send those feelings into the dark. Let them just pour out of you until you feel as if you are empty. Allow the darkness to surround you, then watch as it transforms. Slowly and gently, it is going to take all of your feelings and turn them into light. Beams of crystalline energy now fill the space where the darkness was, reaching for you, ready to fill you up with energy, hope, purpose, and healing. With each breath you take, this new light energy flows into you, making you feel courageous and light as a feather. This is yet another magical way the darkness is crucial to your daily life. So wherever you feel out of sorts today, give it to the darkness—let it transmute, repair, and restore you.

December 24

Many enjoy preparing for family gatherings around this time of the year as the holiday season is in full swing in most parts of the world. Not everyone will celebrate the same holiday or do it in the same way, and some won't celebrate anything at all. Whatever we choose to do, all of us can enjoy the energy of light that permeates the darkness at this time of year. Light is often a large theme this time of year: there are tree-lighting ceremonies, light parades, and all sorts of other activities that honor this festive season filled with lights. And all of this can only happen because of the darkness, which allows the light a canvas on which it may take shape. At this time of year, there seems to be no end to the imagination where light is concerned. Now that truly is a gift, and you can accept today if you so choose.

December 25

Every year, this day can cause some people happiness, others stress, and some pain. In other words, it brings both darkness and light not only to yourself but to many others in your life as well. Your angel wants you to remember that today is just a day like any other. Remember that it's not the day itself that makes people feel the way they do: it is the value, importance, and meaning placed upon it. You can make today mean anything you want. If you want it to mean comfort, wrap yourself in that feeling. If you want it to mean joy, wrap yourself in the feeling of joy. If you want it to mean peace and stillness, wrap yourself in those feelings. Use however you want to feel as a way of engaging with others today. You may make someone else feel more comfort, joy, or peace. How you feel can change the way you experience the darkness, and today is no exception.

December 26

This is your last week of exploring the theme of darkness. Over the course of this chapter, you have explored many ways to use, imagine, heal, and work with the darkness in your everyday life. As you move through your day, your angel wants you to decide how you will allow the darkness to be your ally: Will you call it to you as a friend, protector, healer, or something a little less powerful? Remember, the darkness does not need to be good or bad. It is what you make of it. So choose. Bend it to your will and command it. Play with all that you learned and explore what it means to master the darkness within you and all around you.

December 27

You are moving closer to the end of the year; one complete cycle of your life is coming to an end. You will never be the person you were this year again, which means there is a version of you ready to be released back to the darkness. This version of you is ready to go back to the darkness that created it so it can be reborn as a new version, one with new life lessons, new skills, new dreams, new hopes, and renewed energy. This process can be done slowly over the course of the next few days. Start by giving back all the things that did not go your way over the last year: the hurt, the pain, the disappointment—let it all slip off you and into the darkness. Next, give the darkness what you would like more of. Hand these dream seeds to your angel and see them planted deep in the darkness so that they can grow and multiply. Let the rest of you dissolve and become one with the darkness, if only for a moment, before the light renews you.

December 28

By now, you have gotten used to calling in your angel of darkness. Inviting it in as you would a friend for a chat. You have gotten familiar with how it feels and what purpose it serves in your daily experience. Knowing this allows you to sink into the temporary nature of your relationship with the darkness; it is not something that stays for long, nor does it linger. It is merely a short-term affair. This means the time you have with the darkness now is limited, intimate, and deeply personal. Think about how that makes you feel and how you can bring that feeling energy into your daily experience. Truly consider what it would mean to have deeper, more connected moments with those around you, knowing that all these interactions are short-term, temporary, and ever so fleeting. This is the gift the darkness brings you today.

December 29

The dark offers you the perfect place to reflect in which you can recall everything that went well over the past year and what didn't go the way you thought it would. Use this moment to give thanks for all of it—all the tears, all the laughs, the ups and downs, and all the days. Without these things, you would not be the person you are right now. This year has changed you, shaped you, molded you, not necessarily in a good way or a bad way, just in an ordinary life way. You could even say it happened in a destined way. Just as the year is destined to end and the darkness will follow the light, so too are you destined to come to an ending, a shift, and a quiet moment to reflect on it all. This is the gift your angel Lailah now gives you. All you have to do is receive it.

December 30

The darkness allows you to step into stillness, into a space where nothing has to happen or be a certain type of way; you just are. This seems like the perfect space to be in as you contemplate the year waiting to be birthed from the darkness of the year that was. Your angel wants you to stay in your curious mind but walk with observer eyes. Drop your expectation into the darkness. Dump your bags of wants and desires at the door. Be still. Expand the darkness around you and watch what dissolves with the passing of time and what sticks around.

December 31

The energy of endings brings with it the energy of hope, that something new will be the balm your heart craves. The darkness offers you hope as you walk out of the year once and for all. Hope is the heartbeat of darkness, the promise the angel Lailah leaves you with as you come to the end of your journey with her. So what are your hopes for the coming year, the coming dawn? What is the light you seek now that you know how to measure it and have clarity around the direction it points you in? As you move through this last day of the year, see how those around you are giving you clues to what comes next. Watch as conversations and exchanges with others open doors to possible newness. And look for a feather to cross your path, a parting gift from your angel to let you know your time in the darkness has come to an end.

Closing Ceremony for the Month

Your time with angel Lailah has now come to an end, for this year anyway. It is time to pack up your altar for the angel of darkness. Wash your magical items, wipe down your altar's surface, cleanse your crystals and tarot cards, and put them away. Remember, also, to wave a smoking herb bundle over the space so that you can cleanse the energy and reset it, making it ready for the next angel. As you clean and reset your altar, say a small prayer of thanks:

Angel Lailah, I thank thee
For staying with me
For never leaving me alone in the dark
Showing me how to feel safe

Wrapping me in your wings
Guiding me
Through the darkness
I am grateful for the lesson of this month
To get my night eyes
Now able to see
Things that felt hidden
Clarity and hope are now mine
Angel of Darkness, our time is now done
For now, I clean and clear this sacred workspace
This altar I cleanse
To honor you
To honor the work we have done.
Thank you.

THE WRAP-UP

Welcome to the end, or the end of this book anyway. You have made it a whole year, met twelve new angels, and learned lessons about twelve specific themes. This has been a big journey touching on all aspects of your life; we know you may need some integration time to take it all in. Thank goodness the angels don't actually go away or have somewhere better to be. They are always available to you, ready and waiting to assist you whenever and wherever you need them. So once you have taken a breath, meditate. Let the lessons of the year sink in along with the knowledge that you can call on the angels you've read about and worked with.

Perhaps you want to revisit some of the work done in specific chapters. Maybe you want to bring these angels into your meditation or even journal with them. However you wish to engage with them, just know they are up for it and happy to be of service. You also have the option of doing everything again or using this book as a bibliomancy tool for the next year. Your journey doesn't have to be a one-and-done trip. How you proceed is entirely up to you.

The angels and I wish you the very best, no matter how you move forward. May your days be blessed with love and laughter. May your path be filled with coins and feathers from the angels.

To Write to the Author

If you wish to contact the author or would like more information about this book, please write to the author in care of Llewellyn Worldwide Ltd. and we will forward your request. Both the author and publisher appreciate hearing from you and learning of your enjoyment of this book and how it has helped you. Llewellyn Worldwide Ltd. cannot guarantee that every letter written to the author can be answered, but all will be forwarded. Please write to:

Leeza Robertson
℅ Llewellyn Worldwide
2143 Wooddale Drive
Woodbury, MN 55125-2989
Please enclose a self-addressed stamped envelope for reply,
or $1.00 to cover costs. If outside the U.S.A., enclose
an international postal reply coupon.

Many of Llewellyn's authors have websites with additional information and resources. For more information, please visit our website at http://www.llewellyn.com.